"You are perfect just as you are."
—Samantha Hess

touch

The Power of Human Connection

by Samantha Hess

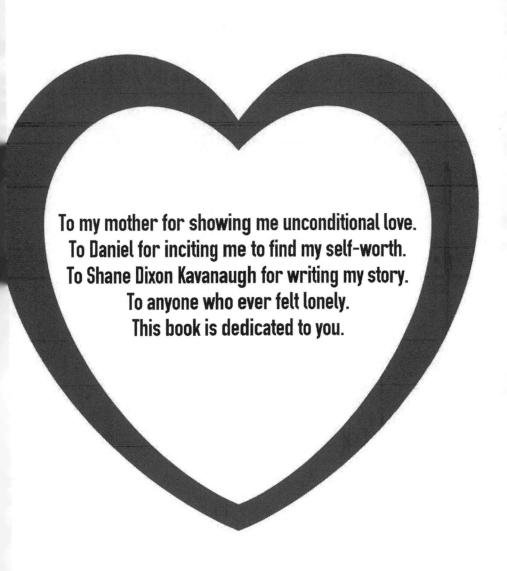

To my mother for showing me unconditional love.
To Daniel for inciting me to find my self-worth.
To Shane Dixon Kavanaugh for writing my story.
To anyone who ever felt lonely.
This book is dedicated to you.

chapters

My name is Samantha Hess.

I am a professional cuddler and I plan to change the world. My service is simple: fully clothed, platonic touch with a dose of unconditional love. Regardless of height, weight, gender, race, occupation, religion or age, I am here to provide the respect and acceptance we all deserve. I created Cuddle Up To Me to provide a safe place for people to receive comfort and encouragement. Some of my clients are divorced or widowed. Others are single. Some are hurt or disabled. Others are autistic. All are welcome.

7

introduction

the end of the beginning

"Your value doesn't decrease
based on someone's inability
to see your worth."
—Lucy Christopher

On a cold September day, my life changed forever. I was working an office job with a team of people I admired. I was 28 years old and married for nearly eight years to my high school sweetheart, Daniel. I owned my car, leased a comfortable condo and had few complaints.

That afternoon, I learned one of the employees I worked with every day died at the age of 38. He left a wife and four children behind. I crawled under my desk and bawled. Eventually, the pain was unbearable and I had to go home. The thought of someone so young passing away was tragic. As I sat in my car waiting for my tears to stop, it dawned on me that life is too short to wait. I thought to myself, if I am unhappy, I must make a change. Today.

My marriage was in trouble and our problems were hardly new. Daniel was my best friend. We got along well and we were a team. Yet something was missing. No matter how hard I tried to find what I needed in our relationship, I came up short. My husband was a good man. He supported me financially, materially and vocationally. When it came to work, I found myself going from place to place, trying to discover my path. I was a housekeeper, hostess, sales associate, floor supervisor, bank teller, youth group exercise instructor, personal trainer, inbound call center representative and an installation coordinator for a security company.

I seemed to be drawn to services all related to making people happy, but the happiness I brought to others was missing from my own life.

Like many couples, Daniel and I faced challenges, but our relationship had many strengths. We agreed on politics and religion. Our communication was clear, and always taking the necessary time to talk through our issues was key. There was not one night where we went to sleep angry. Over time we learned each other well enough to avoid pressing buttons. We listened to each other and waited our turn to speak. We learned early on not to bottle anything up.

The thorn in our relationship, I eventually discovered, was a lack of touch. On every other level, Daniel and I matched perfectly, but we were complete opposites with respect to our need for touch. I was insatiable, desiring warmth and affection at every opportunity. Daniel, on the other hand, could happily take his dog to a cabin in the woods and live in isolation for the rest of his life. His fierce independence was the hole in the boat, and we were taking on water fast. No matter what I said to help him understand my needs, he did not get the message.

"I want you to hold my hand when we sit on the couch," I said. He initially agreed — and occasionally remembered without being prompted — but minutes later he pulled away. The cold chill of the graveyard wind whistled between us. I sought his attention over and over again. Occasionally he made an effort, but within days or weeks my requests went unfulfilled. I asked for his attention a hundred different ways. I described why our connection was important to me. "When you sit next to me, but don't touch me, it makes me feel unwanted and alone — like I don't have a partner," I said. "I need you to touch me every day because that is how I receive love. I need to feel we are connected — and for me that means physically. When we sit on the couch next to each other, but completely ignore one another, we might as well be in different countries. I need more touch from you."

Daniel let me down. There was never enough intimacy. "I feel rejected, isolated, and unloved." I said. "I can't accept this. I need you to do more. I don't feel like I'm asking too much, do you?" I made specific requests. "I would like for you to hold my hand at least two hours a night while we watch television. Can you do that for me?" He routinely agreed but rarely followed through. I became bitter. I was alone on top of a mountain, completely isolated. "Is it really that difficult to hold my hand? Am I so gross to you that holding my hand offends you in some way? Why is this so hard for you? Am I really asking too much from you? I can't take this anymore!" Daniel was my husband. My partner. His inability to make me feel wanted broke my heart. His inability to touch me sent our marriage into a downward spiral.

We were on a trial separation as I explored my feelings, but when I learned about the death of my coworker I saw clearly that my marriage was over. No matter how hard we tried to find a balance that worked for us, he could never fulfill my need for touch. I knew this issue placed our marriage on life support. Life is too short to feel unfulfilled. My need for touch is the foundation of how I experience acceptance. More than anyone, he was supposed to offer love and support. His rejection was too much to bear.

I invited Daniel over the night my coworker died. He probably thought I was going to give him the "second" chance he felt he deserved for the umpteenth time. I told him about my coworker. I told him it finally clicked that no matter how hard he tried I would never be completely fulfilled. I told him our marriage was over.

He was devastated. He never thought I would leave. He had no idea how much pain he caused me over the years. He sat in silence for a long time. Then he got angry. He wanted to yell, but lacked the power to speak. He made no sound. His expressions changed over and over like the marks of a pen from a sketch artist, slowly bringing the final product into view. He broke down. He cried and begged me to take him back. He wanted another chance, but it was too late. In our 13 years we never had a breakup, but this day was our day of reckoning. Ending my marriage was the hardest decision I ever made, but I know in my heart it was the only option. I had to give myself a chance at happiness. This was the only way. After spending nearly half our lives together, it was finally over. I was on my own again.

I had to discover what it meant to meet my needs on my own terms. To find the balance I was searching for I had to figure out what I wanted from life. What did I need to feel whole? Social scientist Abraham Maslow theorized that human needs were arranged into a hierarchy of five basic categories. First, there are physiological needs like oxygen, water, food, shelter and other essentials. Next comes safety needs like employment and property. Then comes our need for love, friendship and sexual intimacy followed by our journey toward self-esteem, confidence and achievement. The final category is called self-actualization, where all of our skills and abilities are used to their highest potential.

As is turns out, Maslow was really onto something. In my marriage, my needs were rarely met. I was surviving not thriving. I was in a rut. My life was mundane; an unimaginative routine. I went years before realizing what I was missing.

Six months before my coworker passed, I woke up with a nagging sense of dissatisfaction. I knew something was wrong. My growing sense of despair became oppressive. Each day offered more of the same. I continued like this for weeks — and eventually months. I was unhappy, miserable and empty. I felt incomplete.

This concept of incompleteness became the light bulb moment I desperately needed. Something was missing, but what? So many of the things in my life were good — or at least acceptable. I had a roof over my head, a hot meal on my plate, transportation, family and friends that loved me. Compared to the troubles people faced all over the world, my challenges felt trivial. There are people without clean water or food. There are hundreds of homeless people camped out within miles of my home. Was I being selfish? Why did I find so little joy in my life when by all outward appearances I was so successful?

This feeling of selfishness drove me toward self-discovery. I needed to find balance in my world, like a newborn giraffe trying to walk for the first time. I was stumbling to grasp onto anything that offered stability, but I had no hands to reach out; only my feet to stand on. With each question my knowledge grew as I put the pieces together. My first step was to identify what might be missing from my life: love, touch, food, sleep, respect, attention, appreciation and self-worth. Over time, I realized all these needs were unmet. My dissatisfaction had no single cause. As Shakespeare noted in Hamlet, "when sorrows come, they come not single spies, but in battalions."

I decided to tackle what I felt was most in my control: food and sleep. Going to bed at a decent hour and eating healthy food went a long way toward making me feel better about myself. It was easier to get up in the morning, smile and make good choices. As my world came slowly back into focus, I could tackle one thing after another. The hardest was self-worth. After years of feeling rejected by a partner who didn't want to touch me, I felt like a tiny mouse inside. I knew how much I did for others, but still didn't think I was worth the same. On one hand, I felt my value to others was very high. Many people counted on me and needed me. On the other hand, how could I be worth anything if the person who cared the most about me wouldn't put forth effort to make me happy?

Ding! Ding! Ding! We have a winner! That was it! That was the answer! At that point in my life my self-worth depended on others. I didn't feel complete unless someone else validated me. What a terrible way to live! When this finally clicked for me I decided to take charge. The shattered person I had become was no longer desolate. My renewal began with looking up inspirational quotations on the Internet and taking direction from anyone who seemed to have it figured out. I plastered these quotes and sayings on sticky notes all over my house, my car and my desk. To this day, I have two affirmations stuck on the door frame to my bedroom: "You've got everything you need right here!" and "Be happy with who you are!"

My confidence returned after a few weeks of this positive lifestyle. I danced, sang and laughed. Life was good and continues to get better! Finding fulfillment in and of myself allowed me to renew my outlook on life. It took me a long time to figure out what was wrong, but once I discovered the fix it was simple. In order for me to feel whole, I had to summon the strength for self-acceptance. I no longer felt worthless if someone else wasn't working hard to please me. I no longer felt rejected or isolated.

Though the collapse of my marriage was painful, I took the opportunity to renew myself. I started from scratch and was in control of my destiny. Life was beautiful again! I felt like myself for the first time in years.

My newfound passion for happiness gave rise to the person I am today. Out of the ashes rose a Phoenix. I was better than ever, ready to explore this new world. It no longer mattered if I had a mate. I was free of the shackles of my depression. Free to do what I wanted, when I wanted and how I wanted.

In January 2013, I ran across an online article with a picture of a gentleman holding a "Free Hugs" sign. He was at a Saturday Market trying to perform a good deed. Another gentleman came along to punk him. He had a sign that read "Deluxe Hugs $2." Apparently the "deluxe hugs" guy got more hugs than the "free hugs" guy. When a dollar value is placed on something we instinctively find it more valuable.

I quickly realized I needed a service that did not exist. Necessity is the mother of invention and I embarked on a career in professional cuddling. In April 2013, with the encouragement of my friends, I bought the domain name cuddleuptome.com and built my site. I can barely post a status update on a social media site, so the task of creating a site from scratch was daunting. Since I am reluctant to shy away from a challenge, I began plugging away. Two months later, I had drafted a client waiver. I launched my Web site (even if it looked like a 12 year-old designed it) and registered my business with the government. After finalizing paperwork with my attorney, I launched my professional cuddling company. No Oregon laws stood in the way of my new venture.

In June 2013, I promoted my business at every opportunity — hanging flyers around town, handing out business cards and posting on social media platforms. I discussed Cuddle Up To Me with everyone I met. By July, my business was off the ground. I was featured in the local newspaper Willamette Week, Their "Best of Portland" issue named me "Best Cuddler (Professional Edition)" which led to a slew of other newspapers, radio stations and media outlets knocking on my door. By November, my story went viral and over 14 million people around the world heard my story! I received supportive e-mails from people on every continent except Antarctica. It may be just a matter of time before some evolved penguin drops me a line. I appeared on CNN, CBS This Morning, NBC News, Fox News, CNBC, AOL, Yahoo, the New York Daily News, the London Daily Mail, Nerve Magazine and dozens of broadcasts around the globe. My media tour promoting this book should allow me to reach roughly 30 million people before the end of 2014.

The publicity my company received is unprecedented in Portland. I am booking clients weeks in advance. My retail cuddling studio launches this year. Public interest in cuddling was so intense I had no choice but to write this book. I needed a way to share my ideas with as many people as possible. With my story reaching across the globe, this was the only feasible way to share my message with everyone.

We all experience moments in life where even our basic needs are not met. We feel lonely, misunderstood, ignored, rejected, overwhelmed or unloved. You are not alone. We all have bumps in the road and professional cuddling lends a helping hand.

My guiding principle is simple. Create a self-perpetuating cycle of positivity. When our personal needs are satisfied, it is easier to help others achieve this same feeling. When we struggle to feel whole, we lack the emotional resources to help others.

When my needs were not met, I felt empty. I served others, but ultimately it was a cry for help. I naively believed that others would look after my needs if I satisfied theirs. Attempting to find fulfillment this way was insincere. I helped others in a veiled effort to obtain support and acceptance. The result was constant disappointment. Too often I felt used, hurt or misunderstood. It took over 20 years to understand and correct my false expectations. I repeated this mistake throughout my life and damaged many relationships. I learned to expressly communicate my needs to other people and I feel fulfilled. My life is now devoted to helping others obtain this incredible feeling of positivity. After reading this book, you will learn to identify your needs, express them openly and find the happiness you seek.

Life is never easy. It requires constant effort. You have the power to control your own destiny. I will help you understand the forces that shape human behavior and dramatically improve your relationships. Take my hand and we will begin our journey to fulfillment.

chapter one

the science & psychology of touch

"I remember that feeling of skin.
It's strange to remember touch more than
thought. But my fingers still tingle with it."
—Lucy Christopher

Touch is essential to healthy relationships. Without the love and acceptance affection provides, my marriage failed and I became miserable. I was determined to understand the biochemical forces unleashed by physical intimacy. I researched the science and psychology behind touch, exploring magazine articles, radio interviews and and videos before graduating to academic papers. It was not enough to "sense" in my gut that touch was vital to our emotional and physical health. I had to do my homework. I had to get in touch with touch.

My research began with the award-winning 2001 documentary "Touch: The Forgotten Sense" by Danish-born filmmaker Kun Chang. The film discussed the impact of tactile sensation on other senses, confirming the relationship between touch and our ability to see, taste, hear, smell and comprehend the world around us. Chang explores the importance of mother-baby bonding and reveals how the absence of touch contributes to emotional and physical deficiencies later in life. In an October 2008 interview with the *New York Times*, Chang said, "People generally don't think about losing the sense of touch because we take it for granted. It has an impact on everything we do."

Our skin is our largest organ and our connection of the intrinsic and extrinsic. This is our barrier, our security system and our gateway to the sensations around us. Our skin tells us if something is hot, cold, wet, dry, sticky, soft, smooth, rough, sharp, slick, greasy, slimy or hard. Touch allows us to comprehend whatever we encounter.

"Touch is the first sense we develop in the human embryo and the last to diminish in old age," continued Chang. "Less than eight weeks after being conceived, an embryo is barely 2.5 centimeters long. It has neither eyes nor ears yet its skin is already highly developed. It is generally believed that the earlier a function develops, the more fundamental it is." Touch is by far our most important sense, essential to our survival and development.

Dale Stack, a psychologist at Concordia University in Portland, Oregon, was a key contributor to the Chang documentary. She revealed the essential role touch plays in nurturing babies. "In the first few months of life and over the first year of life, touching is a very important ingredient — it is extremely important, even essential in the first few days and weeks of life," said Stack. "Touch has an effect on other systems. For example, when the baby is placed on the mother's breast following birth, the suckling on the breast allows for the uterus to contract. Secondly the baby suckling at the mother's breast will affect the milk that the mother's breast is producing — and what I mean by that is that there will be more milk produced and for longer periods of time the more the baby sucks." Developmentally, our bodies would physically fail without the ability to obtain nutrition — what most doctors call "thriving." Touch is our most important sense on an evolutionary scale.

"When we massage premature babies, they gain approximately 45-50% more weight, they are discharged approximately six days earlier from the hospital," said Director Tiffany Field of the Touch Research Institute. "At the end of the first year, they are still showing a weight advantage and at that time they are also doing better on mental scales and motor scales of the I.Q. Test for babies. When we have done these studies we have tried to keep the stimulation to just touch so we will know what touch does. If we were talking and making funny faces we would not know what is contributing to the weight gain. We did a cost-effectiveness analysis because, of course, hospitals want to know if this is going to save any money. We found that if you massaged the 470,000 preemies who are born in the United States you would save $10,000 per preemie because the babies go home six days earlier. If you multiply that by 470,000 you would save $4.7 billion dollars. That is a lot of money."

It is a common misperception that we have only five senses. In reality, we have additional powers of perception, many of which are related to touch. In a July 2011 syndicated article by Karl Smallwood called "Six Lies About the Human Body" I learned not to trust what they taught us in grade school:

Scientists still aren't quite sure of exactly how many senses you have, or what even constitutes a sense but you'd be hard-pressed to find one who believes you have five. Depending on how they count them, they usually wind up with something like 14 to 20. The five you learned about in school were just the five most evident senses, aka the boring ones you could have figured out for your own damn self. The rest are far more interesting. The Harvard School of Medicine lists six extra ones that are pretty hard to argue against. Close your eyes, then touch your nose with your index finger. How did you know which one was your index finger without looking at it? How did you know where your nose was? Did you smell your finger to your nose? Did your sense of touch somehow tell you what the air molecules you encounter along the way to your nose feel like? Nah, that's proprioception, your body's awareness of where it is in relation to itself. It's also worth noting that this sense your kindergarten teacher failed to mention can operate like a freaking superpower. If you're walking in the woods and a bear growls in the bushes behind you and to your left, the bear's growl hits your left ear a millionth of a second before it hits your right. Your sense of time is able to pick up on that infinitesimal difference and allows you to perfectly triangulate the bear's location behind you. If you were only relying on your sense of hearing, you would only know that the bear is somewhere on the left side of your body. Your ears don't swivel around like a dog's, so you would have to turn and use your eyes to pinpoint the bear. A blur of brown and black fur would be the last sight you ever saw.

Without our sense of touch, our other senses are limited or less effective. We *feel* sound before we hear it. We *feel* the rush of heat behind a burning door before we see the flames. Our sense of touch informs nearly everything we perceive.

"There was a study conducted with newborns between five hours and 79 hours," said Stack. "The mothers of these babies were able to recognize their own babies solely through the sense of touch. What I mean by that is that they were blindfolded and were not allowed to use any visual or olfactory cues. Solely by touching their [infant] on the back of the hand they were able to identify and recognize their own babies." Touch plays a critical role in our early development and extends our understanding of the world far beyond what our other senses could achieve.

In the early twentieth century, affection toward babies was viewed with disdain. Doctors including Granville Stanley Hall, Luther Emmett Holt and John B. Watson wrote popular books discouraging parents from holding their children. In her January 2013 *Huffington Post* article "Too Much Mother Love: Proving the Necessity of Nurture," sociologist Lisa Wade claimed these child rearing theories changed the way adults viewed children. "We put adolescents to work in factories and coal mines," wrote Wade. Her article also focused on breakthroughs in experimental psychology that transformed our understanding of the need for physical touch:

> In the sixties, psychologist Harry Harlow did some of his most famous experiments using Rhesus monkeys. He set about to prove that babies needed more than just food, water and shelter. They needed comfort and even love. While this may seem stunningly obvious today, Harlow was up against widespread beliefs in psychology. The need for these experiments reveals just how dramatically conventional wisdom can change. The psychologists of the time needed experimental proof that physical contact between a baby and its parent mattered. Harlow's experiments were part of a revolution in thinking about child development. It's quite fascinating to realize that such a revolution was ever needed.

The Harlow primate experiments were controversial but revealing, confirming that physical touch is a higher priority to infants than nutrition and other vital needs. In an academic paper called "The Science of Love: Harry Harlow & the Nature of Affection," psychologist Kendra Cherry discussed the impact of his research on our understanding of behavioral science:

> In a series of controversial experiments conducted in the sixties, Harlow demonstrated the powerful effects of love. By showing the devastating effects of deprivation on young rhesus monkeys, Harlow revealed the importance of a mother's love for healthy childhood development. His experiments were often unethical and shockingly cruel, yet they uncovered fundamental truths that have heavily influenced our understanding of child development. Many of the existing theories of love centered on the idea that the earliest attachment between a mother and child was merely a means for the child to obtain food, relieve thirst, and avoid pain. Harlow, however, believed that this behavioral view of mother-child attachment was an inadequate explanation. Harlow's most famous experiment involved giving young rhesus monkeys a choice between two different "mothers." One was made of soft terrycloth, but provided no food. The other was made of wire, but provided food from an attached baby bottle. Harlow removed young monkeys from their natural mothers a few hours after birth and left them to be "raised" by these mother surrogates. The experiment demonstrated that the baby monkeys spent significantly more time with their cloth mother than with their wire mother.

Equally compelling was a secondary experiment Harlow conducted confirming the essential role mothers play in helping infants overcome fear:

> Harlow demonstrated that young monkeys would also turn to their cloth surrogate mother for comfort and security. Using a strange situation similar to the one created by attachment researcher Mary Ainsworth, Harlow allowed the young monkeys to explore a room either in the presence of their surrogate mother or in her absence. Monkeys in the presence of their

mother would use her as a secure base to explore the room. When the surrogate mothers were removed from the room, the effects were dramatic. The young monkeys no longer had their secure base to explore the room and would often freeze up, crouch, rock, scream, and cry. While many experts derided the importance of parental love and affection, Harlow's experiments offered irrefutable proof that love is vital for normal childhood development. Additional experiments by Harlow revealed the long-term devastation caused by deprivation, leading to profound psychological and emotional distress and even death.

In a May 2010 article in *Scientific American*, Katherine Harmon detailed the emotionally numbing effects of physical isolation on orphans:

> The stark institutional isolation prevalent in the orphanages of some countries might have mostly melted away decades ago, but many babies and young children all over the world still grow up in environments where touch and emotional engagement are lacking. Many children who have not had ample physical and emotional attention are at higher risk for behavioral, emotional and social problems as they grow up. These trends point to the lasting effects of early infancy environments and the changes that the brain undergoes during that period. Below the surface, some children from deprived surroundings such as orphanages, have vastly different hormone levels than their parent-raised peers even beyond the baby years. For instance, in Romania in the 1980s, by ages six to 12, levels of the stress hormone cortisol were still much higher in children who had lived in orphanages for more than eight months than in those who were adopted at or before the age of four months. After the country opened up in 1989, children weren't interacting with one another as much. After they were adopted into Canadian homes, the longer they had been in the orphanage, the more likely they were to have longer-term [cognitive and emotional] deficits.

London Daily Mail writer Julie Wheldon noted in November 2005 that failing to cuddle infants may have irreversible consequences: "It may come as no surprise to parents, but cuddling your baby provides them with social benefits for years afterwards, according to scientists at the at the University of Wisconsin-Madison. They found a clear link between love and attention in the early years and healthy emotional responses in later life. Children who have been deprived of physical contact as babies have lower levels of social-bonding hormones, the researchers found. Even if they are then smothered with love as toddlers, it can be very difficult to repair the damage. The scientists said their findings may help explain why children who have suffered neglect may struggle to form secure relationships when older."

Children who grow up without physical affirmation face many challenges. If warmth and intimacy are essential to our development, physical and sexual abuse during childhood has a crippling effect on human potential. The Child Welfare Information Gateway published "Understanding the Effects of Maltreatment on Brain Development" in 2009, a definitive report on the relationship between abuse and the deterioration of cerebral function:

> Babies' brains grow and develop as they interact with their environment and learn how to function within it. When babies' cries bring food or comfort, they are strengthening the neuronal pathways that help them learn how to get their needs met, both physically and emotionally. But babies who do not get responses to their cries, and babies whose cries are met with abuse, learn different lessons. The neuronal pathways that are developed and strengthened under negative conditions prepare children to cope in that negative environment, and their ability to respond to nurturing and kindness may be impaired . . . Prolonged, severe, or unpredictable stress — including abuse and neglect — during a child's early years is problematic. In fact, the brain's development can literally be altered by this type of toxic stress, resulting in negative impacts on the child's physical, cognitive, emotional, and social growth . . . Physical abuse can cause direct damage to a baby's or child's developing brain.

Child Welfare Information Gateway researchers observed that abuse and neglect had a number of specific consequences for the victims including learning disabilities, persistent or involuntary fear response and the inability to form emotionally healthy relationships with other people. Their report further concluded that "Infants or children who are the victims of repeated abuse may respond to that abuse — and later in life to other unpleasantness — by mentally and emotionally removing themselves from the situation. This coping mechanism of dissociation allows the child to pretend that what is happening is not real." In other words, harmful touch can compel people to construct alternate realities as a coping mechanism.

According to a 2006 report issued by the National Child Traumatic Stress Network, the long-term consequences of physical abuse are devastating:

> Children who are physically abused can develop child traumatic stress. They are also at risk for depression and anxiety. Child abuse has been linked to poor physical, emotional, and mental development . . . Experts in the field of child behavior believe that physical abuse teaches children to be submissive, fearful or aggressive. It also teaches them that hitting is a way to control other people or solve problems. The attitudes, beliefs, and behaviors that grow out of physical abuse can cause a child to have problems at school, at home, and with friends. Sometimes children who have been hit don't do well at making and keeping friends. They may not trust people in authority. Children may also become fearful of their parents.

It can be confusing for children when a parent, the person they depend on and love the most, hurts them in some way. Being hit may make children feel angry, helpless, powerless, hostile, guilty, or ashamed. It may result in their becoming chronically anxious or depressed. All these negative feelings about themselves increase children's stress levels and only make it harder for them to behave well.

According to the American Humane Association, more than six million complaints of physical abuse against children are filed every year with child protective service agencies across the United States. Touch is so powerful that harmful touch can destroy the human spirit, setting the stage for a lifetime of dysfunction and disappointment with little hope for improvement.

Uncovering the impact of harmful touch compelled me to take action. In addition to writing this book and sharing what I learned about the power of human connection on media platforms across the globe, I joined the Baby Leland Foundation in Portland, Oregon to protect infant children from abuse and neglect. I also volunteer for the Oregon Food Bank to help feed economically vulnerable families. My non-profit work is a vital part of what drives me to succeed. Supporting a non-profit organization that mirrors your values is a beautiful way to contribute. I encourage everyone I meet to volunteer for charities in their community that protect children and families. We can all make a difference.

Positive touch is life-affirming and transformative. Our bodies respond to physical stimulation and my mission in life is to educate people about the power of human connection. The rewarding impact of physical touch is not theoretical. It is confirmed by vast oceans of empirical research.

"Researchers are discovering that the deep pressure applied during massage is a major stimulus to the central nervous system," said Chang. "It sets off a number of reactions in the body. It slows down heart rate, decreases blood pressure, diminishes stress hormones and increases the number of immune cells. Touch, they are finding, is a very powerful stimulation."

In a 2005 *BeliefNet* article titled "The Health Benefits of Touch," Lain Chroust Ehmann identified some of the innovative approaches regional hospitals are employing to include touch as a tool for treating patients suffering from a variety of ailments:

> Because of the positive overall results that touch has on the body, researchers investigated using touch as a treatment for a variety of medical complaints. In a 1998 study on the efficacy of touch for improving functional ability in elders with degenerative arthritis, researchers at the University of Wisconsin (Eau Claire) discovered that touch improved pain,

tension, mood, satisfaction and hand function. Research conducted at St. Margaret Memorial hospital in Pittsburgh showed that another type of touch therapy, called "therapeutic touch," in which practitioners move their hands above the surface of the body and barely touch the skin, eased the pain of osteoarthritis . . . This type of touch may stimulate the body's energy field in a way similar to acupuncture. Dr. Mehl-Madrona says that massage and other touch therapies are thought to have a positive impact on autism and attention deficit disorder in children, resulting in greater relaxation and less acting out. He has also researched the effect of touch on asthma and uterine fibroids, both of which respond well. Dr. Mehl-Madrona sees touch therapy as one of the treatment methods that anyone with a chronic illness should consider. Study after study indicates that touch has a beneficial effect on our perception of pain, treatment of disease, and emotional and physical development.

In a January 2011 article titled "Touching Makes You Healthier," Norine Dworkin-McDaniel revealed how touch provides a powerful health boost, from preventing diseases to defeating hypertension:

"Touch is shaping up to be the ultimate mind-body medicine. From lowering blood pressure and heart rate to increasing immune function and relieving pain, getting touched or doing some touching makes you healthier — not to mention happier and less anxious . . . [it] causes muscles to unclench, a racing heart rate to slow, heightened blood pressure to fall, and levels of the stress hormone cortisol to drop. In that relaxed state, your body is able to regroup and recharge. One happy result: a more robust immune system. "Cortisol suppresses the immune response," explains Roberta Lee, MD, vice chair of the Department of Integrative Medicine at Beth Israel Medical Center in New York City. "Anything that increases the relaxation response triggers the restoration of your immune response."

"Research shows that physical affection has measurable health benefits," wrote Diana Spechler in an April 2013 column for *Oprah Magazine*. "Stimulating touch receptors under the skin can lower blood pressure and cortisol levels, effectively reducing stress. One study from the University of North Carolina found that women who hugged their spouse or partner frequently (even for just 20 seconds) had lower blood pressure, possibly because a warm embrace increases oxytocin levels in the brain. Over time, lower blood pressure may decrease a person's risk for heart disease."

In August 2005, *The Independent* writer Roger Dobson cited a study further demonstrating the stress alleviating effects of physical touch. "Researchers from the University of North Carolina told couples they would have to give speeches. Before they did so, 100 of the couples sat holding hands for a short time, then they embraced for 20 seconds. Another group of couples rested quietly and were separated from their partners. During their speeches, heart rates and blood pressure rose twice as high in the second group compared to the hand-holders."

The benefits of touch are profound and measurable. Biochemical processes are unleashed that ease stress, boost our ability to fight infections and viruses, accelerate the healing of damaged tissue, lower blood pressure and create a feeling of calm. Dworkin-McDaniel identified the specific hormone touch releases that fuels our sense of well-being and improves the way we interact with other people:

> The act of embracing floods our bodies with oxytocin, a "bonding hormone" that makes people feel secure and trusting toward each other, lowers cortisol levels, and reduces stress. Women who get more hugs from their partners have higher levels of oxytocin and lower blood pressure and heart rates, according to research done at the University of North Carolina. But a hug from anyone you're close to works, too. Researchers at the University of Wisconsin at Madison tested that when they analyzed stress levels among volunteers giving a presentation. Afterward, participants who got hugs from their moms saw decreases in cortisol levels an hour after the presentation.

Even something as simple as taking the hand of your partner can ease anxiety, decrease pain and stimulate reward centers in the brain. Dworkin-McDaniel cites empirical data that confirm the biochemical benefits of touch:

> Twining your fingers together with your one-and-only is enormously calming. James Coan, PhD, assistant professor of psychology at the University of Virginia, discovered this when he administered functional MRIs to 16 married women while telling them they might experience a mild shock. The resulting anxiety caused the images of their brain activity to light up like Christmas trees. But when the women held hands with one of the experimenters, that stress response subsided -- and when they held hands with their husbands, it really quieted down. "There was a qualitative shift in the number of regions in the brain that just weren't reacting anymore to the threat cue," Coan says. Even more intriguing: When you're in a happy relationship, clasping hands reduces stress-related activity in a brain area called the hypothalamus -- which lowers the levels of cortisol coursing through your system -- as well as in the part of the brain that registers pain, which actually helps keep you from feeling it as much.

Dworkin-McDaniel also cites sex as a powerful tool in enhancing health:

> Lovemaking involves total-body contact. All that skin-to-skin stroking (not to mention orgasm!) floods us with oxytocin and feel-good endorphins that do wondrous things for our emotional well-being. Regular sex also does the physical body good, possibly even preventing us from getting sick as often.

People who had sex once or twice a week had 30 percent more infection-fighting immunoglobulins in their saliva than those who didn't do the deed as often, according to a study done at Wilkes University in Wilkes-Barre, Pennsylvania.

Portland Relationship Center Marriage Counselor Norene Gonsiewski wrote an online essay in July 2011 about the relationship benefits of cuddling:

> Sex is wonderful for a marriage, but cuddling is what helps couples stay together for a lifetime. Intimate cuddling provides more than sensuality but also the feelings of comfort, security and companionship. Research shows that cuddling releases the bonding hormone oxytocin, which makes couples feel relaxed and safe which in turn opens up more emotional sharing. Couples who cuddle more, feel more bonded and that connection creates attachment. Attachment helps couples to look out for one another, rather than hurt one another. It is more difficult to hurt a partner with whom you feel connected . . . Oxytocin is so successful at creating connection, that a couple can spend twenty minutes cuddling before a serious discussion about kids or money and avert conflict.

If you are not receiving the love, acceptance and physical attention you desire in a relationship you are not just compromising your emotional comfort; there are verifiable consequences for your physical health. Missing out on touch weakens you over time. Without physical intimacy from friends and loved ones we become sick, stressed and demoralized. Just as a flower needs water and sunlight, people need love and touch to blossom.

In 2005, *Time* published an article by Michael Lemonick titled "Health: The Biology of Joy," revealing how negative feelings harm our physical health. University of California, Berkeley psychologist Dr. Dacher Keltner observed that depression lowers cortisol levels and suppresses immune function resulting in higher susceptibility to illness. He also noted that painful emotions "can worsen heart disease, diabetes and a host of other illnesses" and that positive emotional associations ramp up "electrical activity in the left prefrontal lobe of the brain." Touch alleviates stress, strengthens our ability to fight off pathogens and stimulates our brains to function at a higher level.

In his 2010 academic paper "Hands On Research: The Science of Touch," Keltner further confirmed the proven health benefits of touch. " In recent years, a wave of studies has documented incredible emotional and physical health benefits that come from touch . . . massage therapy reduces pain in pregnant women and alleviates prenatal depression — in the women and their spouses alike," said Keltner. "Research here at UC Berkeley's School of Public Health has found that getting eye contact and a pat on the back from a doctor may boost survival rates of patients with complex diseases . . . This research is suggesting that touch is truly fundamental to human communication, bonding, and health."

In February 2012, *Prevention* writer Siobhan O'Connor revisited the positive impact cuddling has on easing the symptoms of depression. "If you look at patients with depression, one of the first things to drop off the map are social interest and social connection," wrote O'Connor. "The oxytocin hormone [released by cuddling] promotes what psychologists call prosocial behavior — being kind, helpful, empathetic, and friendly, among other things — it may just be an antidote to the alienation experienced by so many people when they're down."

In her article "Cuddle Chemical Oxytocin Relieves Alcohol Withdrawal," *Time* writer Maia Szalavitz revealed that cuddling helps people with addiction issues. "The love hormone oxytocin can relieve symptoms of withdrawal in people recovering from alcoholism," wrote Szalavitz. "Oxytocin was found to help dramatically. Those given the hormone required nearly five times less lorazepam to get through detox, compared to those on placebo. They also had less anxiety. The research was led by Cort Pederson of the University of North Carolina at Chapel Hill and published in *Alcoholism: Clinical and Experimental Research*."

Keltner calls touch "our richest means of emotional expression" and an emerging wave of research confirms that truth. In a February 2010, *New York Times* article titled "Evidence That Little Touches Do Mean So Much," Benedict Carey cites several examples:

> The evidence that such [touch] can lead to clear, almost immediate changes in how people think and behave is accumulating fast. Studies have found that students who received a supportive touch on the back or arm from a teacher were nearly twice as likely to volunteer in class as those who did not. A sympathetic touch from a doctor leaves people with the impression that the visit lasted twice as long, compared with estimates from people who were untouched. Research by . . . the Touch Research Institute in Miami found that a massage from a loved one can not only ease pain but also soothe depression and strengthen a relationship. In a series of experiments led by Matthew Hertenstein, a psychologist at DePauw University in Indiana, volunteers tried to communicate a list of emotions by touching a blindfolded stranger. The participants were able to communicate eight distinct emotions, from gratitude to disgust to love, some with about 70 percent accuracy.

In 2009, Keltner cited research confirming that physical contact improves our character. "Touching triggers trust and generosity. In one study, participants were asked to sign a petition in support of a particular issue of local importance. Those participants who were touched when asked to sign signed 81% of the time. Those who were not touched during the request volunteered to sign at a rate of 55%."

An article in *Good Housekeeping* by Ayana Byrd from February 2012 confirmed that cuddling even makes you smarter. "Researchers at the University of Miami had people do a difficult math problem, then had them do it again after receiving a chair massage. Post-massage, subjects showed increased speed and accuracy in solving the problems as well as more pleasure in the task, thanks to the reduction of stress."

In a 2009 *Big Think* lecture, Keltner explained how humans evolved to improve our sense of touch and the essential role touch plays in our ability to form lasting bonds:

The science of touch is just getting off the ground and in part because western European cultures tend to be low-touched cultures. We don't touch as much as people in other cultures and, you know, it, first of all, taking a Darwinian evolutionary perspective on it, we, as we lost our hair for thermoregulation purposes, our skin became amazingly rich with all kinds of neurons and networks of receptors to process information of different kinds of touch. And then we evolved this amazing hand which is different than other primate hands and it's very dexterous and does a lot of great things, and what the science is showing and, it is stunning, is that when I receive a very friendly form of touch, you know, a stroke to the arm, a pat on the back, it releases oxytocin, a neuropeptide that promotes trust. It shuts down stress-related parts of the brain like the amygdala, and the locus coeruleus, it activates a branch of the nervous system we study called the vagus nerve, which is involved in connection and by the way, the vagus nerve controls your immune system in part as well, new science suggest. There are a lot of studies now, dozens showing that warm friendly touch increases weight in premature babies, reduces signs of depression in Alzheimer's patients. It's preventative medicine.

In 2009, Keltner wrote a landmark book called "Born to Be Good: The Science of a Meaningful Life" where he identified touch as "the first language we learn" and suggested human goodness has biochemical origins. "We are made of neurotransmitters as well as regions of our nervous system that promote trust, caring, devotion, forgiveness and play," said Keltner. Physical touch releases oxytocin, a chemical that accelerates our ability to form social bonds, making touch an essential building block in the development of whole societies. "We know that touch builds up cooperative relationships," said Keltner. "It reinforces reciprocity between our primate relatives, who use grooming to build up cooperative alliances."

On a personal note, I loved reading an April 2008 *Michigan Online* article by Jodi McFarland about a deep-touch pressure device called a "hug vest" created by students at Saginaw Valley State University. It is designed for autistic children and wraps around their upper torso, increasing their sense of security by releasing the hormones serotonin and dopamine. Their prototype is now on track for production and promises to improve thousands of lives. Dozens of commercial devices employ "deep-touch" pressure therapy for patients including a body-sized "squeeze machine" developed by Dr. Temple Grandin in the early nineties. Several of my clients have mild to severe autistic tendencies. Having a safe and comfortable environment where they are in control of the touch they crave allows them to make so much progress in their lives. It's quite — excuse the pun — touching.

It is no coincidence that boxers who retreat to their corner during a match get rubbed down and massaged by their trainers. In addition to soothing tired muscles, they express emotional support that helps their fighter prevail. Athletes and teams that touch each other routinely boost their performance. *New York Times* writer Benedict Carey cites a study by Michael W. Kraus and a research team "that coded every bump, hug and high five in a single game played by each team in the National Basketball Association . . . with a few exceptions, good teams tended to be touchier than bad ones. To correct for the possibility that the better teams touch more often simply because they are winning, the researchers rated performance based not on points or victories but on a sophisticated measure of how efficiently players and teams managed the ball — their ratio of assists to giveaways, for example. Even after the high expectations surrounding the more talented teams were taken into account, the correlation persisted. Players who made contact with teammates most consistently and longest tended to rate highest on measures of performance, and the teams with those players seemed to get the most out of their talent." The study concluded that touch enhances athletic performance by reducing stress. "A warm touch sets off the release of oxytocin, a hormone that helps create a sensation of trust and to reduce levels of the stress hormone cortisol," said Carey. "In the brain, prefrontal areas, which help regulate emotion, can relax, freeing them for . . . problem solving."

One of the obstacles to increasing the amount of physical attention we receive is cultural. Keltner cited a study from the sixties confirming America is a touch-deprived culture compared to countries like France and Puerto Rico:

> Some Western cultures are pretty touch-deprived, and this is especially true of the United States. Ethologists who live in different parts world quickly recognize this. Nonhuman primates spend about 10 to 20 percent of their waking day grooming each other. If you go to various other countries, people spend a lot of time in direct physical contact with one another — much more than we do. This has been well-documented. One of my favorite examples is a study from the 1960s by pioneering psychologist Sidney Jourard, who studied the conversations of friends in different parts of the world as they sat in a café together. He observed these conversations for the same amount of time in each of the different countries. What did he find? In England, the two friends touched each other zero times. In the United States, in bursts of enthusiasm, we touched each other twice. But in France,

the number shot up to 110 times per hour. In Puerto Rico, those friends touched each other 180 times! In the United States, people . . . seldom touch each other, while in Europe and South America, people . . . touch each other frequently . . . Of course, there are plenty of good reasons why people are inclined to keep their hands to themselves, especially in a society as litigious as ours. But other research has revealed what we lose when we hold back too much . . . Our cultural emphasis on individuality seems to make us less happy than folks in cultures that emphasize compassion and group solidarity.

In a massively popular November 2013 *Good Men Project* article titled "The Lack of Gentle Platonic Touch in Men's Lives is a Killer," writer Mark Greene argued that gender roles limit the amount of physical attention American men experience, harming their health and isolating them emotionally:

We believe that men can never be entirely trusted in the realm of the physical. We collectively suspect that, given the opportunity, men will collapse into the sexual at a moment's notice. That men don't know how to physically connect otherwise. That men can't control themselves. That men are dogs. Accordingly, it has become every man's job to prove they can be trusted, in each and every interaction, day by day and case by case. In part, because so many men have behaved poorly. And so, we prove our trustworthiness by foregoing physical touch completely in any context in which even the slightest doubt about our intentions might arise. Which, sadly, is pretty much every context we encounter. And where does this leave men? Physically and emotionally isolated. Cut off from the deeply human physical contact that is proven to reduce stress, encourage self-esteem and create community. Instead, we walk in the vast crowds of our cities alone in a desert of disconnection. Starving for physical connection.

In February 2006, *Emotional Intelligence* blogger Kathleen Keating discussed touch deprivation and the inhibitions that prevent people from physically bonding:

We are suffering in our society from a sad condition best described as touch deprivation, skin hunger and hug inhibition. We need to recognize that every human being has a profound physical and emotional need for touch. We are alone in our separate bodies, yet to live we must connect with each other in order to belong and get our needs met. Touch is the primary way we contact and connect with each other. Touch is the experience of how I meet you and you meet me and we meet the world. We touch the world, and the world touches us. Touch is a contact function. We meet the world outside of ourselves, outside the boundary of our skin, we make contact with the boundary of our skin. Our skin is the antennae that feels, touches, contacts the world. With touch, we meet the world outside of ourselves in a vibrant, alive, nourishing way. With touch we meet, connect, bond and belong.

Touch is especially essential to our psychological well-being due to the isolating effects of modern technology. We can instantly reach each other from every corner of the earth, but something is lost in translation. Busy lives create patterns of behavior that discourage intimacy. Despite mobile phones and social media profiles, we are more disconnected than ever before. Technology makes communication effortless, but somewhere along the way we lost our footing. We invest disproportionate amounts of time interacting with friends and family on digital screens. Our lives are increasingly two-dimensional. Even when we make personal contact, we are constantly interrupted by calls and messages. The tactile interactions we have are increasingly hard, cold and impersonal. This book is an effort to bring us closer together, improve the ways we communicate and discover the intimacy we need to thrive. It is time to rediscover the power of human connection.

"We are humans passing by each other all day long, often without ever really connecting, everyone knee-deep in their own life," wrote *Huffington Post* Columnist Chrissy Kelly in a February 2014 essay. "Many of us [are] simultaneously busy and bored all at once. Most of us have so much in common and we don't even know it because we are afraid to put ourselves out there. The single mom, the working parent, the parent of a child with special needs, the stay-at-home mom or dad — we all feel lonely and think it's because of our circumstance, but I think it's a trait we all share. If we can tell the honest truth about how we are feeling, we can create beautiful and real opportunities to connect."

"We are losing the something grand and mysterious that makes us compassionate," said Keating. "We are so much more profoundly complex than machines, it is ludicrous to make a comparison, as we often do, when we use machine metaphors. Like machines we have skills — but we must not imitate machines. It is essential to stay connected to the divine animal in each other. Touch is our primary connection. With touch we are restoring the balance in those human qualities that are far more powerful than 'machine' skills. We are all committed to a better understanding of love and it is one of the greatest tragedies of our day that our culture often equates tenderness with weakness and love with sentimentality."

"As we spend more time at the computer, in the office, or on business travel, we have increased stress and fewer opportunities for physical contact," wrote *Beliefnet* columnist Lain Chroust Ehmann. "Even when people are face-to-face, concerns about sexual harassment and inappropriate touching can make people overly cautious and reluctant to touch each other. As a result, many of us may find ourselves starved for ordinary, casual touch from our acquaintances. One simple way to improve your quality of life is to incorporate more touch into your daily activities. Something as simple as hugging family and friends hello and goodbye can help put them — and you — in a better frame of mind and may even provide a boost to physical health as well. And with virtually no negative side effects, a good dose of touching may be just what the doctor ordered."

In a 2009 *Big Think* lecture, Keltner took these concerns about technology even further, arguing that the digitization of social interaction represents a step backwards for human evolution:

> As evolutionary scientists we . . . think about behaviors that help us survive and help us reproduce . . . One of the truisms in the study of attraction and falling in love and finding a person you would eventually have offspring with is you have to be in their physical presence and it promotes that. I asked my undergrads recently, you know, as a rhetorical question, how many of you have fallen in love with somebody, or are actively in love with someone, and in a relationship with someone you've never been around physically, and a third of the class said yes. And the little evolutionary part of my brain said, well, good luck reproducing on that. In the context of our hominid evolution thousands of generations, we evolved in these small groups and to the best of our knowledge from studies of hundreds of gathered cultures and archaeology, the sense is that we were always in face-to-face, skin-to-skin contact and that led to the evolution of facial muscles and exquisite receptors in the skin and eye contact . . . It raises a really interesting question about what we are losing in our more remote world. I think there is a sense we're losing a good deal. We certainly are losing skin-to-skin and face-to-face.

Over the past 50 years, social scientists created mountains of data confirming the relationship between touch and successful human development. Without the positive physical touch and comfort of a mother, we become fearful, reluctant and imbalanced. As adults, physical intimacy is essential to our well-being. I am determined to educate people about the vital role touch plays in our world. It is the focus of my career. If I can persuade hundreds of thousands of people to discover or rediscover the power of human connection, I can change the world and help people feel whole. This is the essence of the cuddling movement. We can reduce unemployment, lower medical costs, extend lives, improve learning, increase self-worth and inspire people to understand their own value. Satisfying our need for physical intimacy is an investment in human potential.

chapter two

communication

"Human speech is like a cracked kettle on which we
tap crude rhythms for bears to dance to, while
we long to make music that will melt the stars."
—Gustave Flaubert

Communication is the art of getting two or more parties to accept the same reality. The goal is to be understood but perception is subjective. People might say one thing but mean another. We hear what we want to hear instead of the actual message. We misread body language. We create judgments from limited data and jump to conclusions more frequently than we should. We assume our family and friends understand us intuitively but accurate communication requires effort. Much of the drama in our lives is self-inflicted. Jealousy, lack of intimacy, trust issues and unrealistic expectations are often the result of miscommunication or misunderstanding.

Most of the people in our lives want us to be happy but they are not mind readers. If they ask us what is wrong and we tell them "nothing" we are being evasive. If something is wrong, speak up or let it go. If a topic is not worth discussing, it is not worth being upset about. Simple as that.

When people ask about our troubles we can avoid drama by replying "thank you for noticing" and calmly sharing our concerns. Instead of brooding, I openly air my feelings. The quicker we pull off the Band-Aid, the less it hurts. We can only bottle our feelings for a short time. Silently fuming causes everyone to suffer. Better to be candid and sincere.

Someone dear to me has a learning disability related to nonverbal communication. No matter how hard he tries, he only picks up on a small percentage of the nonverbal communication most of us rely on to understand each other. I am Italian, and nonverbal is huge for me. I initially had a heck of a time finding balance with him. He is bright but unable to pick up on most social cues. Finding ways to clearly communicate with him is helping me learn new and unique ways to interact with everyone around me.

When we say things like "I'm thirsty" or "We've been inside all day, it sure would be nice to go for a walk" we expect the person we are with to offer a glass of water or take us outside for a stroll. These are statements, not requests, and the people who hear them may not understand our requests when delivered in this manner. Miscommunication happens because we think we are being perfectly clear, but the other person misses the hint. They are not being dumb, dense or lazy. They simply do not understand we are requesting something from them. This is our own fault. Their inability to "read" us does not diminish their affection or dedication. There are many aspects to effective communication and in the coming pages we will discuss many of the ways you can improve the communication in your life.

Listening

"All truths lie waiting in all things. They unfold themselves more fragrant than roses from living buds, whenever you fetch the spring sunshine moistened with summer rain. But it must be in yourself. It shall come from your soul. It shall be love."
—Walt Whitman

I love the old saying "We have two ears and one mouth so we can listen twice as much as we speak." I definitely believe in this concept. Most of us think we listen more than we actually do. Instead of truly listening, we spend this time thinking about what we are going to say next. We miss information when we focus on our rebuttal instead of the words spoken to us. Yes, we may "know" what someone is saying or where they are going with their train of thought, but giving them our full attention and actually allowing them to say things in their own way, in their own time, will allow for much more effective communication overall. Because our perceptions don't always match reality it is best to be patient and let someone speak freely, even if we know everything they are going to say. If they are choosing to take the time to say it, we should be respectful enough to hear it.

I'm sure I'm not the only one who has said to someone on the street "What a beautiful day!" only to hear "I'm fine, and you?" in response. We hear what we want to hear, or at least what we *perceive* someone might say based on our expectations. If we fail to focus, we miss the intent behind what is said. Listen first, and let your conversation partner know if you need a moment to reply. Over time, the people around you will learn to be patient as you formulate your thoughts. Hopefully you will be comfortable doing the same. Insecurities in that moment of silence are fleeting and will help avoid most miscommunications.

The more that I practice active listening, the more I realize I need to be a better listener. Listening is like a muscle, it must be worked out on a regular basis to maintain strength. Allow yourself to be humbled by your listening skills, and you may find there is more to learn that you realized. Try some of the listening exercises below to give your skills a real workout.

Listening exercises:

Finish my sentence
With a partner, take turns saying the first part of a sentence and having the other person finish it for you. This will strengthen your bond as you listen and laugh. It will allow you to learn things about how the other person thinks, feels, and reacts to the world around them for a better understanding of each other. Here are some examples to get you going. Feel free to make them up as you go along:

I went to the park and . . .

My dream vacation is . . .

The silliest word I can make up is . . .

When all else fails . . .

The ultimate robot would have . . .

If I made a movie it would be about . . .

Follow the Leader
In a safe environment (no stairs, sharp objects, etc.) blindfold your conversation partner. The goal is to guide them using only verbal communication to a spot that requires several commands to reach. This works well going from a bedroom to the living room or from a tree to a bench in the back yard if you are brave enough to go outside. Once you reach the spot safely, switch roles. The goal of this exercise is the same as using GPS; if you listen carefully you will safely reach your destination.

Listen Between the Lines
Think of something you want your partner to guess. It could be a music artist, a food item, something in the room, etc. Set a timer for whatever time you need: 15, 30 or 60 seconds depending on the item you are choosing. The person listening then starts reading something: a book, a magazine or status updates on a social media site. Start the timer and describe your item without using any part of the word or rhyming. Take turns and see how much each of you can pick up on while multitasking. This exercise is meant to show you how difficult it can be to carry on a conversation with someone who is distracted. Many of us do this

every day, but when you do this as an active game you will start to notice how a distraction like reading your email while holding a conversation can complicate communication.

Guided Meditation
A guided meditation is any verbal description meant to visually stimulate someone while allowing them to find a calm and centered focus. A guided meditation might involve walking someone through slow-breathing exercises while relaxing different body parts or describing a perfect day on the beach. Take turns with your partner giving a guided meditation on any imaginable topic. Make your verbal imagery vivid. Be creative and have fun. There is no wrong or right way to do this, but it helps to clear the room of distractions including pets, noises and so forth. When I do this, I try to let each person speak for 5-10 minutes at a time. No need to set a timer, just describe the images in your head using words and calming tones. Only introduce serene, beautiful and pleasant ideas into your guided meditations. The goal is to shut off any distractions and immerse yourself in the vision. You will feel relaxed and positive in no time, especially if you do this while cuddling.

Verbal Communication

"Do not dwell in the past, do not dream of the future, concentrate the mind on the present moment."
—Buddha

Learning to speak words that allow others to fully understand what we are trying to say is tough. It requires the right tone, tact and tenacity. While we may be speaking the same language, we each have our own unique spin on it. We create inflection and have our own pace. According to the *Global Language Monitor*, there are a million words in the English language and new phrases are created every day. That's a lot to learn. Not to mention a whole spectrum of slang to keep up with. Two years ago I had never heard the term "meme." A few weeks ago, I found out that "YOLO" means You Only Live Once (yeah, I know, I missed the train on that one).

When it comes to verbal communication, I like to encourage a very simple philosophy: Say what you mean, and mean what you say. Many of us are reluctant to verbalize our needs because we fear not getting what we want. We guarantee as much by saying nothing. If you want something, ask for it. Read that last sentence again. The worst that can happen is someone tells us no. Better to take a risk than to fail for lack of effort, provided our requests are reasonable.

When my little sister learned she was pregnant with my nephew, she said she was more afraid to tell me than our parents. She was young and the father was not going to be in the picture. I'll admit I was harsher and more judgmental than I should have been, especially since she needed my support. My sister was born to be a mom. She is amazing with her family and I am more proud of her every day.

Her reluctance to tell me about the baby was a shock. She was filled with self-doubt and I quickly realized I was being insensitive. My behavior made her fear I was unsupportive. Luckily, my baby sister forgave me and allowed me to remain involved despite my initial reaction. She was a portrait of grace and civility, a trait she developed over time. My nephew Eli is a great kid which I attribute to having a great mom. There was no need for me to be upset. The circumstances of her pregnancy were distressing but I always knew she was smart and capable.

Growing up I caused situations that created unnecessary drama with my sisters, family and friends due to my harsh and immediate emotional response. I am determined to be less reactive in life. When I respond to events in a positive way, people around me feel more secure. We all experience tough times. Shocking news can trigger strong reactions. If unchecked, our response can hurt people we care about. We need to accept people for who they are. People deserve to be heard and taken seriously. Understanding others is made possible by listening, not jumping to conclusions. If we want someone to give us the benefit of the doubt, we must show them courtesy and respect. Finding the right words to achieve desired results is effortless when the people we are speaking with listen attentively. Try some of these exercises to improve your verbal communication:

Verbal Communication Exercises

Public Speaking in the Shower
Remember the classic trick of picturing the audience naked to help you stay calm while speaking to a group? This exercise is the opposite of that. Instead of speaking to a group, try giving your speech while you in the shower. Pick a topic that you know well. Voice the unpracticed speech to front of your grooming products and see how the flow of words changes as you rework the dialogue over a few days. The more you do it, the easier it gets. In time you will see improvement in the flow of everyday conversations.

Turn Back Time
We all have moments we fret over. Moments where we needed a perfect line to really drive home our point. Mine are usually when I am talking about my business. Professional cuddling is not a concept people easily understand. I have to practice my answers over and over to get it right. Think of occasions in your life when you needed to persuade someone: convincing your boss to give you Friday off, getting a friend to babysit or haggling over the price of a car. Replay those exchanges in your mind and imagine what you could have said differently to secure a better outcome. Try saying your practiced answers out loud on your way home from work or write them down for reference later. When we train ourselves to create the perfect response, we will have the right words on the tip of our tongue when that next opportunity arises. Be confident, diplomatic and prepared. Practice makes perfect.

Improv Night

Gather a few friends for an improv night. Have everyone write down a few different scenarios: romance on the moon, dog at a burger stand or the best concert of all time (take turns shouting out the next scene). Have two or more people "on stage" where they have some room to act. To get started set a timer (two minutes) or try a key word (pineapple!) to stop the act so you can tag in. The only required rule is you must all agree to accept any requests made while in the scene. Any other rules (like nothing sexual, anything said must to in the form of a question, or no physical contact) are up to your group to decide. Keep things fun and lighthearted. As you practice your improv skills you are learning how to verbally communicate in a quick and efficient way.

Nonverbal Communication

"Treat people as if they were what they ought to be and you help them to become what they are capable of being."
—Johann Wolfgang von Goethe

We say so much without saying anything at all. The *Nonverbal Group* blog confirms that most communication occurs nonverbally:

> One of the most frequently quoted statistics on nonverbal communication is that 93% of all daily communication is nonverbal. Popular science magazines, students and media outlets frequently quote this specific number. Dr. Albert Mehrabian, author of "Silent Messages" conducted several studies on nonverbal communication. He found that 7% of any message is conveyed through words, 38% through certain vocal elements, and 55% through nonverbal elements (facial expressions, gestures and posture). Subtracting the 7% for actual vocal content leaves one with the 93% statistic. Nonverbal behavior is the most crucial aspect of communication.

There are innumerable ways we communicate without spoken language — a look of love, open arms, smiles, frowns, tense shoulders or a wink. People around us are often more aware of how we feel than we are. As intuitive creatures, we pick up on minute details without even trying. We can tell if someone is tired, stressed, happy, scared, sad, excited, nervous or anxious. Nonverbal communication is the same as the intent behind the written words in a book. It gives us a deeper sense of what is being said.

In order for us to communicate accurately, our verbal and nonverbal messages should match. We need to be able to sincerely convey our intentions. My ability to hide my true feelings is almost nonexistent. I wear my heart on my sleeve and I don't like hiding how I feel. You always know where you stand with me because I have spent almost zero time practicing hiding my feelings. It has gotten me in trouble from time to time.

Last Summer I went camping with a group of friends. We went to Lake Chelan which is this picturesque little town about six hours north east of Portland. My friend, affectionately known as Captain, spent every summer at Lake Chelan since he was a child. I was honored to be invited along. He explained that we would be "princess camping," and I assumed that meant there would be showers and outhouses. I didn't realize it meant hot showers, clean public restrooms with amenities like soap and mirrors or big grocery stores within walking distance. The whole town was so perfect it looked like a scene from a movie, minus the cameras. Gorgeous!

Instead of being grateful for the conveniences of the camp, I asked the first question that came to mind: Was there a way to make a fire? I could tell my friends regretted bringing me for a moment when they replied that no fires were allowed at the campgrounds. For me, the beach girl, camping without a wood fire was a devastating blow. I scowled. My expressions revealed what a whiner I was! Looking back, the trip was so amazing that not having a campfire proved unimportant. I got to share a week of my life with a group of friends I now call my second family.

The bond we created once I got past my issues was phenomenal. These people are forever in my heart because they helped me learn so much about myself. Nonverbal communication is even more important than the words we speak. If you would like to improve your nonverbal communication skills try some of these exercises:

Nonverbal Communication Exercises

Funny Faces
Take turns using your facial expressions to create an emotion and have your partner guess what you are trying to convey using no words or sounds.

Touch of Emotion
Grab a blindfold and find a comfortable spot for this exercise. Similar to funny faces, sit with your partner and try to convey an emotion just by touching only hands. Emotions like: anger, love, surprise, or gratitude are good ones to try out. Switch and see how many emotions each of you can guess correctly.

Staring Contest
Because eye contact is a huge part of nonverbal communication, having a staring contest helps us become more comfortable with the act. In this exercise, sit in a comfortable position facing your partner. Once you start there is no talking or looking away, though blinking is acceptable. See who can go the longest without looking away. It may be harder than it seems.

chapter three

how to say no and yes

"Communication leads to
community, that is, to understanding,
intimacy and mutual valuing.
—Rollo May

Our desire to make others happy is often the reason we say yes. Many of us say yes regardless of our own considerations. From a young age, it is instilled in us to make others happy. As children we are taught to obey. This leads to guilt when we say no as adults. The desire to make people happy can make it hard to say no. Some have learned to say no without the negative side effects many of us experience. If you pay close attention, you can identify people in your life who mastered this skill. It certainly takes practice and effort. For me, learning to say no was quite a feat. It is still something I struggle with occasionally in my personal life.

As an inherent people pleaser, my goal is to make others happy. My friends know they can call me if they lose their keys (day or night), need a donation to meet their fund raising goal or their car battery dies. I am happy to help. Anytime people in my life want or need something, I do my best to offer support. No reciprocation is expected. Only a "thank you" is required.

My word is my most valuable possession. If I say I'm going to do something, you better believe I will do everything in my power to make it happen. "Integrity, honor, respect and love" is my motto. People know they can count on me.

When you have a generous spirit, people sometimes take advantage of you. This is not necessarily on purpose, but it happens. Many of my friendships suffered because I am a giver, not a taker. On the flip side, I have a ridiculously hard time asking anyone to do anything for me. Over time some of my friendships became imbalanced. The longer I allowed things to continue down this path, the less chance there was for the relationship to succeed long-term. I felt used, disrespected and unimportant to the people I allowed to treat me this way. I believed if they truly cared about me, they would want to do as much for me as I do for them. This mindset was counterproductive as it led to the imbalance I sought to avoid. I was the one teaching them how to treat me. They did nothing wrong. They had a need and they sought to fill it by asking for help. What a concept! For me, this reality was hard to accept. You mean it is okay for me to just ask when I need support? Seems pretty straightforward, right? For many of us this concept is foreign. We are independent. We rely on ourselves. We work at our own pace. When we ask someone else for help we feel out of control. We have to wait for results. As we pass the baton, we fear we are no longer in the race. We get anxious and sense something is missing.

After years of repeating this cycle I found a way to stop it. I can just say no. When I don't have the time, energy or desire to accomplish whatever is asked of me I can politely decline. I can prioritize time for myself. When my life is in balance, I become a better person. Like everyone else, I need help from time to time. Saying no gives me room to be relax, negotiate a workable schedule and not feel overwhelmed. I am no use to anyone if I barely have time to eat or sleep.

As a professional cuddler, boundaries are extremely important. If I don't voice my concerns immediately I risk harming my reputation, hurting my business and losing customers. If I allow someone to get away with something slightly inappropriate—even once—it encourages them to test boundaries. It diminishes the therapeutic aspect of what I do and ushers in a less-than-platonic mindset. Many of my clients ask specific questions before they touch me. It can be uncomfortable telling them no, but my ability to answer clearly and quickly allows the issue to fade. If they ask if they can put their hand on my posterior I say no. If they ask if they can touch my lips, I say no. All behavior must remain completely platonic. With the techniques described in this chapter, you will summon the confidence and power to say no and feel good about it as I do.

Ways To Say No

Below are approaches I take to saying no on a regular basis. Having these ready in your back pocket will make you feel much more prepared and give you an easier way to achieve the desired result while still maintaining your relationships and sanity.

Go-to No
It is easier for me to say no to something if I have a go-to phrase. Try a few options and see what best fits your personality. Your go-to no is perfect for

rejecting treats in the office, party invitations, favors from friends and requests you lack time to complete. I highly encourage an "excuse-free no" as your go to response. It is a quick and easy way to get on with your day.

Excuse-Free No

We often overcomplicate our responses when saying no. Don't feel guilty about being vague. A simple answer is sufficient most of the time. Going out of your way to explain yourself is not going to change the outcome. Keep it simple with phrases like "no thank you" or "not at this time." There are endless possibilities, but keep it short and clean. The less wordy your answer, the quicker you can move on.

Alternative No

There are times when I may want to say yes but just can't make it work. In these scenarios, I try offering a different solution. An Alternative No is great to have as an option for anyone who regularly asks you more than you can reasonably give. Try out a few options and start finding agreements that work better for you. Some examples:

"No, I'm not free Tuesday. How about Thursday?"

"No, my finances are restricted at the moment but I can donate some time."

"No, I can't take Eli all weekend, but how about Sunday afternoon?"

Postponed No

If you are unsure whether you can help someone, try a postponed no. Some examples:

"My schedule changed. I have to postpone our weekly game for now."

"This project is taking longer than expected. I will call if I am available to help."

Transfer the Blame No

When an excuse for saying no is required, it is useful to transfer the blame to someone or something else to avoid negative feelings. I am not saying you should falsely cast blame. Find a truth that works and go with it. Blame your workload. You might not feel well. Make sure your excuse is sincere.

"No, I can't make it. My calendar is crazy at the moment."

"No, I would love to join you for pizza but I'm allergic to oregano. Yes, it's a thing."

"No, I won't be able to make it to the concert. I work in the morning."

Reconfirmed No

Some people just can't take a hint. When we say no, we mean it. There are people who will not let up and dealing with them is frustrating. Don't let these people get under your skin. Keep your cool. They think they can wear you down. Show them they are wrong. It is totally acceptable to say no. You have a choice. My trick with these people is to speak in a quieter and softer voice each time they ask. If you are unflappable and force them to truly listen they will eventually accept your response.

The Rule No
Friends often attempt to borrow money, videos, books and other items that go unreturned. I find using the "rule no" is the perfect way to get out of giving up something you don't want to surrender while still maintaining a positive relationship. When you tell someone "Sorry, but I have a rule where I don't lend this out" that will usually end the discussion. If they continue to question you, reconfirm your answer with an "excuse-free no." You already gave your excuse with the rule. Sharing more can trip you up, providing an opportunity for them to persuade you. If you change your response to a "yes" you are setting up a dynamic that will allow the situation to happen again. If someone asks for something once, they will likely ask again. Stick to your guns and avoid this relationship faux pas the first time.

Practiced No
It never hurts to rehearse your delivery when you plan to turn down a request. Mentally review what you intend to say. Practice makes perfect. More than our words, nonverbal communication creates the impact we desire. Think about your tone, inflection, stance, eye contact and facial expression. Spend time thinking about what you need to convey.

How to Ask for What You Want

You just learned how to say no. Now let's discuss how to ask for what you want. If you are like me, giving comes naturally, but taking feels wrong. It is rare that I am asked for more than I offer because I make it my job to anticipate needs. I inherited this trait from my mother. She would make each one of us four kids something different for dinner at our request. We certainly took advantage. On the same night she might make burgers, grilled cheese and spaghetti all before she went to her second job. No matter what we asked for she served us with a smile on her face. We were completely unappreciative. It makes me cringe to think I was such an awful child. I've learned by watching my mother's endless love and nurturing that we can have a positive impact on others. Her selflessness taught me to balance my ego with humility. She taught me that giving to others is a more rewarding gift than focusing solely on ourselves.

My ability to sense what people need comes from watching my parents. They ensured our every need was met. Their selflessness came at a high price. It was excruciating to watch them suffer through aches and pains, constant stress, weakened immune systems and chronic fatigue. Decade after decade, they gave every ounce of themselves to support us.

The love I have for my parents, and the lessons they taught me, reach deeper than any ocean. I learned that thinking of others without consideration for your own happiness can eat away at you. We should still serve others, absolutely. The "golden rule" need apply. You will suffer in mind, body and spirit if your needs are not met too. There must be balance.

This is where asking for what you want is essential. When push comes to shove, our goal is success not survival. To thrive, we must reach out and utilize our community. Artists rarely paint with one color. They use a palette of colors and create a masterpiece. Each of us is a color. When blended together the result is extraordinary. Red needs blue to make purple. We must work together to enhance our lives.

Knowing what to ask for from others can be difficult. For some of us these requests are effortless:

- Will you scratch my back?
- Will you get me some water?
- Can I have that?

I have a hard time asking for something if I can do it myself — but that is the fun of it. Do you remember the old Goofy Gopher cartoons? The Mac and Tosh method of giving and getting is great! They were incredibly polite, constantly asking if they could do something for the other. Mac might offer Tosh food, and Tosh might offer Mac the opportunity to attack their enemy. They were extremely gracious and polite. "After you" said Tosh. "No, after you," replied Mac. Their synergy was priceless. This is the type of interaction that makes asking for something easier. If you desire balance and plan to ask for more in your life, explore some of the concepts here.

Determining What to Ask For

This is the process I employ to assess whether what I am asking for is appropriate. Follow along with a paper and pen and get ready to try these out!

1) What was asked of me?

Focus on what people requested from you in the past. Here are some examples:

- car rides
- food
- drinks
- baked goods
- massages
- hugs
- cuddles

- donations
- the time
- advice
- clothes
- books to borrow
- babysitting
- gum

2) If I was completely selfish what would I ask for?

Think in terms of what you actually want, not what you think is appropriate. Write it down. Indulge in this guilty pleasure. Here are a few examples of mine:

- So much cuddling!
- Someone reading to me
- Massages
- Someone touching me 80% of the day
- Surprise day trips to somewhere fun

3) What do I feel comfortable asking for?

Now that you know what you want, consider what is reasonable. The answer may be different depending on who you ask and how well you know them. For practice, request something from different people in your life including a family member, friend and a romantic partner. Write down at least two things to ask for if the opportunity arises. My examples:

My Mom
- Recipes
- Art advice
- Super long hugs!

My boyfriend
- Cuddle time!
- A butt/leg massage (innocent and amazing!)
- More affection (always!)

A friend
- Company for a night out dancing
- A hiking buddy
- Life advice

Performing these three steps can provide ideas when opportunities arise. Now comes the hard part.

How to Ask

When determining how to structure your request it can be difficult to find the right approach. Here are eight tips to ensure your request creates a positive result:

Be Direct
The easiest way to get what you want is to simply ask. Be efficient in your request and do not throw in any explanations as to why you want something. Ask plainly. Try something like this:

- Would you . . .
- May I . . .
- Are you up for . . .

The Compliment Request
Sometimes it feels easier to ask if we butter up the person we are asking. Be genuine and heartfelt with your communication. This is handy if you are concerned about getting a yes. Some examples:

"Sunshine, you are my strongest friend! I can't think of a single person I know who is stronger! Would you please help me move?"

"Mom, you are the most talented chef I know! Can I have your chocolate cake recipe?"

"Hey Prince Charming! You are the sweetest person! Would you help me make 100 cupcakes for my nephew's birthday party?"

Avoid open-ended questions
An open-ended question may end in aggravation due to the lack of commitment required. Be specific to ensure your request will actually come to fruition. Very specific. In the end, this will avoid a miscommunication and heartache. Here are the ways to modify your question to avoid confusion:

Wrong: Can we go to the beach sometime soon?
Right: Can we go to the beach this Saturday and leave before noon to avoid traffic?

Wrong: Will you hug me more?
Right: Can we work out a way to ensure that I get at least four hugs a day?

Statements before questions
Some people need to understand *why* we need something before we ask for a favor. It may be helpful to precede the request with a quick explanation. This should not be something that inspires guilt. Manipulation is never positive. Be candid, sincere and brief in your explanation. Some examples:

"Touch is how I receive love best, and it would mean a lot to me if we could incorporate more touching in our lives. I would like to propose we spend an hour cuddling before bed on weekends. Is that something you would agree to do with me?"

"Between school, work and kids, Paul and I never have any time alone. I want to plan a surprise night out for the two of us. Would you please watch the kids Friday night?"

Be confident
When you ask for something it is easier for someone to turn us down when we are shy or meek. Be confident when making requests. Believe that if you ask, they will deliver. Never frame your question pessimistically or concede you think they will say no. Let them decide for themselves if it is something they are willing to do. This does not mean you should be rude or demanding. Just avoid being a pushover. Here are some examples of how ask questions with confidence:

Instead of saying:
You are probably too busy, but I was wondering if you will be able to walk the dog after dinner?

Try saying:
I need you to walk the dog after dinner. Will you take him to the park for 10 or 15 minutes please?

Instead of saying:
I know you will probably say no, but I was thinking maybe we could go to a concert Friday night. If you're too busy it is okay, but I thought I would just see. Are you free?

Try saying:
I know you have a busy week, but it would be thrilled if you came with me to this concert on Friday. Can we make this happen?

Don't Ask For Too Much:
We know when we are being reasonable. We certainly know when someone is asking too much of us. If I have a pent up need to ask, it is important I do not request too much at once. When I make many requests in a small amount of time — even if I have not asked for anything in a very long time — it comes across as unreasonable. We train people how to treat us. It is imperative that we moderate our requests over time. When I have a drastic change in my needs, it may put the other person in a defensive state. I may act in a demanding way due to built-up resentment. When assessing whether a request is appropriate, I try to recall what they have requested of me in the past. If someone asked for shoulder rubs it should be acceptable for me to ask for the same. If someone asked me to prepare a meal, they could certainly return the favor. If the request is along the same lines, do not be afraid to ask someone to reciprocate an equivalent action.

No Whining, Demands or Ultimatums:
When you are fed up with someone taking advantage of you, the communication to resolve the issue can be explosive, like shaking a soda before opening the top. Do your best to avoid letting your bottled-up emotions out at once. Try to start a conversation when you first sense the problem.

Other people may not understand our needs. This is not their fault. No one can read our minds. If we are clear in our communication and ask direct questions, people usually honor our requests. Whining, demanding and issuing ultimatums negatively impacts your relationships. Be kind, calm and sincere in your requests.

Be Prepared for a No
We often do not ask for something because we fear the answer will be no. Be prepared for this possibility. How we handle disappointment is a measure of our character. If we look betrayed or angry when someone says no it may damage the

relationship. As adults, being told no should not be a big deal. If you are asking for a kidney, sure, you can feel devastated. Otherwise be cautious with your response. Resentment is a sign of immaturity. When the answer to our request is no, let it go. *Really* let it go and be okay.

Saying no to others once in a while gives you time to find yourself in the chaos of everyday life.

chapter four

touch

"And I sometimes think that a moment
of touching is the difference between complete
utter despair and the ability to carry on"
—Eleanor Cameron, "The Court of Stone Children"

A gentle caress, a warm embrace, a longing hug, tiptoeing fingers or a comforting nuzzle — we all have different ways we want to be touched. Our desires constantly change. We want what we want, when we want it and how we want it — but we are unlikely to fill you in on the specifics. We are afraid to ask for what we want which leads to unmet needs. We could take a lesson from the Cat Handbook, lessons I observed from living with felines most of my life:

Cat Handbook

Rule #1: When you want attention, ask for it.
Rule #2: If they aren't getting the right spot, tell them.
Rule #3: Vocalize what makes you happy.
Rule #4: Balance your need for touch with plenty of independence.

We fear we will be judged if we ask for what we want and with good reason. This happens frequently — in our heads. We need to break down barriers within us. We interfere with our own happiness. No matter how much we are loved or understood, the people close to us are not mind readers. We must ask for what we want or miss out.

I am a touch-driven person almost to a fault. I don't just want touch — I need it. When I am touch-deficient I feel incomplete, unloved, sad and unmotivated. Touch drives most of the interactions in my life. This chapter explores positive ways to obtain more intimacy. My goal is to help you improve your satisfaction in life by exploring the power of touch.

Who Should We Touch

As we discovered in Chapter 2, we owe our very existence to touch. Yet we live in a world where many of us are afraid to reach out and connect with people around us. Boundaries are fundamental for society to function and it is important that we follow basic guidelines to ensure the safety and comfort of others. That being said, we need more platonic touch. In my life, I touch as many people as I can. It is important to read body language, and not to push personal boundaries, but a quick touch on the shoulder is rarely inappropriate. Verbal and non-verbal cues are essential to understanding the boundaries of personal space. When I meet someone for the first time, they usually extend their arm for a handshake. From a distance, I extend my arms to signal I would prefer a hug. If they mirror my stance I go for the hug. If they do not, I take it as a sign they are uncomfortable with my request and I match their gesture with a handshake instead. Everyone has limits. Some people resist intimacy. This does not require you to limit platonic interactions with the rest of the world. Who we touch comes down to two questions: Who am I comfortable touching? Who do I feel comfortable asking to touch? This is different for each of us but I encourage you to think in broad terms. There are many types of touch and if you explore your options you can find something appropriate for almost anyone.

Guidelines

Circumstances:

My first consideration when it comes to touch is the situation. Am I out dancing? At the DMV? In line at the grocery store? Next I consider who in this situation I have a reason to touch and why. Am I trying to slow dance with my boyfriend? Am I handing paperwork to the person at the counter when I go in to renew my license? Am I trying to reach the gum next to the person in front of me in the checkout line? Finally I consider whether a touch from me might be perceived as inappropriate, unwanted or unwelcome. If the touch I want to give has potentially negative consequences, I make additional judgments to assess whether to proceed.

Types of Touch:

There are endless reasons for touch so I like to take into account the type of touch I am seeking to give. Everyone has their own guidelines for appropriate touching. The scale I use on the next page is a helpful assessment tool. If my levels do not make sense for you, create your own guidelines. Use your own best judgment.

STRANGERS	ACQUAINTANCES	FRIENDS	FAMILY	ROMANTIC PARTNERS
LEVEL ONE	LEVEL TWO	LEVEL THREE	LEVEL FOUR	LEVEL FIVE

Examples of Level One Touch
- Handshakes
- Quick arm touches
- High-fives

Examples of Level Two Touch
- Handshake using both hands (one on their arm)
- Quick shoulder/elbow touches
- Two-second plus shoulder touches

Examples of Level Three Touch
- Quick hugs
- Two-hand shoulder touch
- Hand massage

Examples of Level Four Touch
- Hugs longer than five seconds
- Back massage
- Face touches

Examples of Level Five Touch
- Kissing anywhere except cheeks
- Sensual actions you wouldn't want your mom to see

Body Language

We learn a lot about someone from their body language. Are they standing tall and confident with a big bright smile, making eye contact with people as they pass? Are they tensed up with a Fred Flintstone neck and a flushed face? Are they breathing heavily and brooding around as if nothing is going right?

People usually provide signs indicating how they might respond to being touched:

Positive signs may include

- Good posture
- Shoulders down and relaxed
- Smiling face
- Feet facing you when interacting

Red flags may include:

- Arms crossed
- Eyebrows scrunched
- Frowning
- Moves to preserve their space

- Eye Contact
- Laughing
- Mirroring your body language
- Relaxed

- Will not give eye contact
- Unhappy sighs
- Closed arms
- Fidgety

Nonverbal Requests:

When I want to touch someone and I do not observe any red flags, I offer a nonverbal gesture like bringing my arms up for a hug, extending my arm for a handshake or raising my hand for a high-five.

Nonverbal requests are a good way to see if someone opposes touch. If another customer is zoned out in a grocery store and I need something in front of them, I move closer to test their reaction before gently placing a hand on their shoulder and saying "excuse me."

With new friends I do the same thing. I test their boundaries to see what level of touch is appropriate. If I open my arms for a hug and they counter by shaking my hand, we probably aren't going to be friends (just kidding). If someone offers a downgraded touch instead of rejecting the idea completely, I am happy to meet their comfort level. Touching people communicates acceptance. Over time I might test their boundaries again. Touching must be a positive experience for both sides for the benefits to hold true.

Verbal Requests:

When you are unsure how someone might react to being touched, the simplest solution is to ask, "High-five bro? May I have a hug please? How much wood would a woodchuck chuck if a woodchuck could chuck wood?" Okay, maybe not that last one, but asking for what you want is a great way to know how comfortable someone feels about being touched. When you practice the verbal communication exercises in Chapter 3 you will have all the tools you need to determine when it is acceptable to touch a stranger's hair, high-five the mailman or pet that adorable puppy someone is walking down the street.

Common Sense:

Unfortunately, common sense is not always common. You have it and I have it but collectively it is in short supply. Knowing whether to touch the right person at the right time requires common sense. Is it okay to lick someone's hand? No. Is it okay to slap your coworker on the bum when you greet them? No. Is it okay to ask your nephew for a hug? Absolutely. Is it okay to ask a stranger for a hug? Maybe. If that stranger is the girl writing affirmations in sidewalk chalk at the park, the answer if probably yes. If that stranger is lurking in a dark alley wearing sunglasses, the answer is obviously no. Just a matter of common sense.

Anticipating the reaction of the other person is crucial in determining who we should touch. There are many reasons why someone may or may not want to be touched. To make successful connections, employ good judgment and be aware of your actions.

When is it Appropriate?

This question is subjective so I encourage you to explore what works best for you. Not every person is going to feel comfortable in every situation. The most important factors are intent and trust. Remember that spoken words account for only a fraction of communication. Consider your intentions and your level of trust with anyone you intend to touch. The comfort of both parties is higher if you are on the same page.

For example, if I am reading emails on my phone while in line at a store, it would be totally appropriate for the person behind me to tap my shoulder and say "She can help you over there." On the other hand, if the person in line behind me is so close that they are touching me with their basket or can smell my hair this is unacceptable because we have no baseline relationship. I never met this person or looked them in the eye. Unless you have some compelling reason, keeping a distance of one or two feet from people around you is the social norm.

Trust is something many of us take for granted. If someone does not trust me I should not invade their personal space. Another consideration is hygiene. I could be the nicest person on the planet but if I have body odor or coffee breath most people will look for an exit. Here are some helpful tips:

- Bathe regularly
- Brush your teeth after meals
- Limit cigarette smoking
- Apply perfume in moderation
- Use cologne sparingly

Many of us are sensitive to strong odors. No one wants to be touched by someone unclean or whose hygiene is offensive.

For those of us who have gone without touch, or are unsure if our touch is appropriate, it can be difficult to get started. If you fit into this category and are unsure of where to begin, I recommend hiring a professional in the touch industry. If you are lucky enough to have a professional cuddler available in your town, they can provide advice and walk you through improving your skills. If that is not an option, hire a masseuse and during your massage focus on the techniques they use to make you comfortable including: speed, pressure, and motion. Try to emulate their technique when rubbing or massaging others for a simple way to improve your sense of touch.

Improvement Techniques for Touching

Take time to understand how others want to be touched. With the techniques described in this book you have plenty of tools to make certain touch is given and received positively throughout your life. Practice makes perfect. Find a willing partner and get to work! In this section we explore different techniques to improve your touch skills:

Hugs

Hugging has one essential rule. Do what feels comfortable to you. If you have a hard time finding people you can ask for hugs, try volunteering at a retirement home. Elders in your community would love to have some company. This can be a great way to obtain the positive touch you seek in your life and to inspire others in the process. There are many types of hugs. Here are a few to try out:

The Church Hug
Stand a foot or two apart and bend at the hips to hug with as little touch as possible.

The Bear Hug
Get close and wrap your arms tight around each other. When you are with the right person don't be afraid to really squeeze. Stand close enough to really get a lot of body contact for this one.

The Ol' Pal
Stand shoulder- to-shoulder and wrap your arm around your pal. The arm doing the hugging can extend to your pal's shoulder or rest on their mid-to-upper back. Your outer hands can meet in front for an epic high-five.

Hand Massage

You don't need any special skills to do a hand massage. Try it out on yourself to get an idea of the pressure to use, but the best rule of thumb is the lighter the better and to ask if they prefer more pressure as you go along. Very soft touches from someone else on your hands feels amazing, and is a comfortable place to touch most anyone. If someone has never experienced a hand massage, tell them how amazing they are and ask if you can give them one. Some people will be apprehensive, but if they agree I am certain they will be happy with the experience. If you are interested in learning hand massage techniques, here are a few to try:

Finger Swipes
Use your fingers to press lightly in a side-to-side motion across the fingers as you work your way to the fingertips. Stop before you reach the nail.

Small Circles
Use your thumb to lightly press in a circular motion on different parts of the palm.

Caterpillar
Use your thumb to inch along their palm as a caterpillar moves across a branch.

The Jig
Grab both hands by the fingertips and dance a little jig when you meet.

Kneading
Use both of your thumbs alternately on the palm to slowly apply light pressure

Handshakes

A handshake reveals a lot about us. This is an underrated use of platonic touch. Have fun with it. Create different handshakes with your friends. This exercise is a great way to bring people together. Some possible handshake ideas:

The Forearm
Go for a handshake, but lightly grab arms and shake elbows instead. Enjoy that delightfully-awkward moment

The FTG
Fist bump with the back of your hands and end with an upward motion as your fingers spread out for an explosive effect.

The Cotton-Eyed Joe
When you meet, have one person place their hand on their hip with the elbow out wide. The other person laces their arm through the space created between the arm and the body to interlock arms as you both skip in a circle.

The Lumberjack
Assume a diagonal stance and grab opposite hands to form an "X" with your arms. Once interlocked, moved your arms back and forth as if you are cutting down a tree

Other Techniques

Tea Time
Invite someone over for tea. Try the "Mac and Tosh" method of serving. By this I mean you fill their cup and hand it to them, and they fill yours and hand it to you. Use small tea cups to increase the number of exchanges. Sharing a warm beverage and passing back and forth allows us many opportunities to touch hands in a safe and appropriate way while releasing the "feel good" chemicals in our body that nourish us.

Drawing Game
Use your partner's skin as your canvas and draw on them. Use different parts of the body to draw different things: a hand to draw a star, an arm to make a

lightning bolt, the back to create a flower pot. Take turns guessing what they are drawing and enjoy the positive effects of touch in a safe and comfortable way.

Cuddling

This is my favorite way to improve your sense of touch. I cuddle with my friends, family, and special guy. I prefer one-on-one cuddle time but definitely enjoy a good group cuddle with my "chosen family" from time-to-time. Watch a movie, listen to soft music, chat or take turns reading out loud. Try collective story telling by taking turns telling a small portion of an epic tale that you make up along the way. People are often unsure of the best way to cuddle or how to get comfortable. This is my chosen profession and I devoted the rest of the book to teaching you how to get started. Continue on to explore the great world of cuddling!

"In poverty and other misfortunes of life, true friends are a sure refuge. The young they keep out of mischief; to the old they are a comfort and aid in their weakness, and those in the prime of life they incite to noble deeds."
—Aristotle

chapter five

cuddle personalities

"I am still determined to be cheerful and happy, in whatever situation I may be; for I have also learned from experience that the greater part of our happiness or misery depends upon our dispositions, and not upon our circumstances."
—Martha Washington

We all want and need different things when it comes to cuddling and touch in our lives. Take the quiz and/or read below to determine which cuddling category best fits your personality. Once you determine your cuddling personality, read the improvement section for your cuddle type to learn how to enhance your cuddle skills. Take the quiz if you want help deciding which category fits you best. Otherwise skip ahead to page 58 to read the cuddle personality descriptions and decide for yourself.

Cuddle Personality Quiz

You need cuddling like:
A) Air (you must have it)
B) Water (you need it)
C) Food (you want it)
D) New shoes (once in a while is fine)
E) A hole in the head (you don't want it)

You like to cuddle with:
A) Everyone
B) Family, friends, and your special someone

C) Only family and your partner
D) Only your significant other (or one specific person)
E) No one

You would cuddle this often:
A) 24/7
B) Daily
C) Once a week or less
D) Once a month or less
E) As little as possible

You most enjoy cuddling while:
A) Just being with the other person
B) Talking
C) Listening to music
D) Watching television/movies
E) Having as much space as possible between you

You are most comfortable being touched:
A) Anywhere
B) Any part of the body that would not be covered by underwear
C) Back, Shoulders, Arms, Hands, Lower legs, and head/face
D) Only shoulders, upper arms, and hands
E) Only hands

While cuddling you most enjoy the positions:
A) That allow you to have eye contact
B) That keep you as close as possible
C) Where your heads are close together
D) That avoid eye contact
E) Where your heads are far apart

Your cuddling type most closely resembles:
A) Roots of a tree (all up in there)
B) Puzzle pieces (a balance of closeness and unity)
C) A bunch of celery (touching, but easily separable)
D) A Cat (moments of closeness, but generally more independent)
E) Apples (touching only where necessary)

Your Cuddle Personality

If you answered mostly A's:
Your cuddle personality will likely match the **Ultimate Cuddle Bug**.

If you answered mostly B's:
Your cuddle personality will likely match the **Outgoing Cuddler**.

If you answered mostly C's:
Your cuddle personality will likely match the **Conventional Cuddler**.

If you answered mostly D's:
Your cuddle personality will likely match the **Cautious Cuddler**.

If you answered mostly E's:
Your cuddle personality will likely match the **Anti-Cuddler**.

Cuddle Personality Descriptions

This section is a description of the most common cuddle types. Each category might not fit every person within it, so take these descriptions with a grain of salt and go with your own instincts about what works for you. As you read through the cuddle personalities think in terms of what you ideally want in your life versus what you currently receive.

Ultimate Cuddle Bug

You are the type of person who just can't get enough when it comes to touch and cuddling. You are known to hug everyone you run into from your neighbors and friends to the cashier at your grocery store. Sitting next to someone you prefer your legs touch, and on the couch there is never an inch between you. If it were up to you, cuddling would happen 24/7.

Outgoing Cuddler

You are the type of person who feels comfortable shaking hands, giving high fives, and hugging your friends on a regular basis. Spending hours at a Saturday market with your friends offering free hugs would not be out of the question, and you consider yourself someone that others would think of when they are feeling down to help cheer them up. You go out of your way to show your appreciation for those in your life through your touch. Whether it be a hand massage and manicure, or walking down the street chatting the day away arm in arm. You show your love through your touch, and feel comfortable giving it freely and often with those that are close to you. Ideally you would get cuddle time from someone every day.

Conventional Cuddler

You consider yourself a cuddler and enjoy cuddle time with your romantic partner frequently. You may have regular hugs and cuddles from a few close friends or family members, but you you cuddles are reserved for special people in your life. You are fine with PDA (public displays of affection) in the form of hand holding or hugs, but prefer to keep long kisses to a private location. Your ideal cuddling situation includes a few sessions a week.

Cautious Cuddler

You are independent and do not seek hugs when you are feeling down. Very rarely will you offer to give a hug, but if someone asks you for one you rarely turn them down. You prefer to cuddle with your partner for short times, but enjoy your space. You wouldn't mind watching a movie with your feet in someone's lap, but being cuddled up close to someone for a whole movie sounds uncomfortable. Your ideal cuddle time would be short bursts one to four times a month.

Anti-Cuddler

You rarely feel the need for physical attention. A quick hug from your mom may be appropriate in rough times, but cuddling is not your thing. You may feel unsafe or anxious when others enter your personal space. If it were up to you cuddling would best be left to baby animals.

For whatever level you are at with your cuddle personality you can improve upon the impact cuddling has in your life and for those around you. Read on to learn how to best improve the touch and translation in your life based on your cuddle personality.

Cuddle Personality Results

Ultimate Cuddle Bugs

If you are the type that is insatiable with your cuddling you probably have a pretty good skill set to call upon when it comes to touch. You know the right places, times, and pressures to use to create a positive and healthy experience with all of those whom you encounter. Because of your advanced skill I would like you to encourage to speak openly to those in your life who may benefit from additional touch in their lives. Help teach them that touch is not a four letter word, and that it can go a long way to enhance their lives. Offer to give hugs, high fives, and encourage simple ways to exchange small touches to help get them comfortable. The best way you can improve your cuddle life is by helping others gain your knowledge.

Outgoing Cuddler

You are fairly skilled in the art of touch, and know how to make others feel comfortable. There still may be times in your life where you are lacking the ideal level of touch you would like to receive. These are going to be times when maybe you have gone through a breakup or lost someone important in your life. Maybe the promotion at work didn't come through, or you have been laid off all together. When these difficulties arise in your life it is so important for you to reach out. Share with the people in your life your situation, or at the very least ask for more hugs and cuddles time. Allow yourself to be comforted by those who care. It can be easy to withdraw yourself and sort of hide for a bit, but honestly when it comes to getting back to good reaching out and finding the support you need to get through will make you bounce back so much faster. Do not allow yourself to struggle alone.

Conventional Cuddler

You have the basics down and are able to fulfill your need for touch fairly easily, but you may still be missing out on positive ways to impact many of the relationships in your life. I would encourage you to work on expanding your comfort zone with who and when you cuddle and touch. When you start to incorporate touch in your life in new ways you may find your desire for touch to be stronger and has more benefits on your overall well being than you have previously thought. Try some of the techniques described in chapter four to really enhance your already positive experiences with touch and cuddling.

Cautious Cuddler

It is likely that you have yet to experience the true joy that cuddling and touch can provide. Many of us are uncomfortable based on a lack of touch from our childhood, possibly negative touch in our lives in some way, or having found mostly people who were not great with their sense of touch and reciprocity therefore leading to unpleasant feelings in regards to tough. You may have one or two people who make you feel good when you are close, but in general you have learned to self-soothe instead of relying on others. I would like to encourage you to spend some time thinking about what has lead to your outlook on touch and thinking of ways you are comfortable with touch and cuddling. When you do experience touch try to stop and think about what was good or bad about the situation and what could have made it better or what made it good. Try experimenting with adding more touch in your life on your own terms and see if it is something that you can become more comfortable with. The more positive experiences you have with touch the more you may find you like it and want/ need it in your life.

Anti-Cuddler

Many of us who do not enjoy cuddling or being close with others find that there has been a lacking in their life or traumatic experiences with touch. Touch is something very personal, and precious. It is something we should always have control over in our lives, but maybe didn't always get. Maybe touch is just not a language you speak. It could be that you grew up with a high level of positive touch in your life, but for whatever reason it is just not something you are drawn to or interested in. Whatever the case may be I would highly encourage you to seek out learning the language of touch. I say this specifically because even if it is not something you need in your life the chances that you will find only people around you who are the same is very limited, and the people around you who are touch people may suffer from this lacking in your relationship with them. For touch driven people when someone does not feel comfortable with basic touch it can be devastating and hurtful to feel the rejection of someone who is never interested in touching. If you are uncomfortable asking the people in your life to help you learn this skill seek out a professional cuddler. They can give you the comfort and safety to learn positive touch and how to incorporate more touch in your life quickly and easily.

"Treat people as if they were what they ought
to be and you help them to become
what they are capable of being."
—Goethe

61

I would like you to share yourself with me — every stitch of you — so that I may be warmed and nourished by your tapestry. And I would not like you to worry that some of your threading is inappropriate or uncomfortable to share with me, because I am only here to accept you exactly as you are and to take interest in the way you step through life.

So lay on me your doubts, your troubles, your faux pas, your suffering, your sadness. Lay on me your hopes, your dreams, your excitements, your curiosities, your guilty pleasures.

I want to see you how you see yourself.

And while you tell me all of this and more, I would like to rest my eyes upon your eyes, and take my hand upon your back, and laugh up to the ceiling as you divulge, because it is in these moments of pure exposure that I bask in the ever-so-specific you, and I become the ever-so-specific me, and even though you've never stepped into the tides of the pacific and I've never ridden a skateboard, I am more sure than I've ever been that we are the same."

—Brentan Schellenbach

chapter six

cuddle positions

"I want to love you without clutching, appreciate you without judging, join you without invading, invite you without demanding, leave you without guilt, criticize you without blaming, and help you without insulting. If I can have the same from you, then we can truly meet and enrich each other."
—Virginia Satir

My intent with including the cuddle positions is to give you some ideas to try. Each position will require a personal touch to make it just right, so feel free to experiment. There is no wrong way to cuddle, and even if what you end up doing doesn't look exactly like the picture rest assured that as long as you and your partner are comfortable, you are doing it right. This chapter includes a legend for those of you who prefer to have a baseline for the who/when/where of cuddling. This is in no way meant to be the end all be all for what will appropriate in your specific situation. There is no way for me to predict what scenarios will work best for you, so following your own instincts is the best route to your success. Many people just have no clue where to start when it comes to incorporating touch in their lives. I want to ensure that everyone has a comfortable starting place when it comes to adding touch. The legend I am providing is generalized, and a great tool if you are looking for some ideas to help get you started.

Remember that we all have different needs when it comes to touch. Many of us don't have a true grasp on exactly what we need when it comes to touch, so don't be afraid to try things out. It took me years and years to figure out that the lack of touch in my life was the driving force behind my weight gain, depression, lack of self-worth, and rejection issues. When you do have a clear picture of what your needs are it's so important to communicate them clearly. Make requests, not demands. Ask for specific things instead of making vague statements, and overall remember that you are respected, accepted, and loved unconditionally for exactly who you are.

When it comes to cuddling I prefer to make the following considerations when possible:

- How long do we have?

- Where will we be?

- How cold/hot will we be?

- Will I be comfortable in what I'm wearing? (something soft and breathable is best, also considering if the clothing will move too much while we're cuddling)

- How is my hygiene? (ie showered, teeth brushed, clean hands, fingernails trimmed, toenails trimmed, legs shaved, facial hair that won't irritate your partner's skin, not too much cologne/perfume)

- How much have I had to eat/drink?

- Should I plan for music, a show to watch or a book to read?

- Do I need to bring anything to make myself more comfortable? (a special pillow, candles, a change of clothes, a snack or some tea)

- Will I have to set an alarm to make it to my next obligation and if so will my alarm sound be pleasant?

- Is the environment we'll be cuddling in conducive to the interaction? (cleanliness, odors, lighting, noise, pets, people)

When a cuddle opportunity happens don't shy away simply because you haven't been able to make additional considerations. Go with what's right for you, and be okay with losing sight of the minute details. When someone cuddles with you they care enough about you to overlook the coffee breath, unshaven face, or that shirt that's on day 3. Try your best to be mindful of the little things, but a quick mention of whatever might bother you or your cuddle buddy should put both of your minds at ease.

In the next few chapters you will be introduced to many cuddle positions that I have narrowed down to the most likely scenario in which the cuddle will happen. We start off with the Modest positions. These are the ones that will be appropriate for most people without much concern for the creep factor. Pay attention to social cues, and always communicate, but in general you should find something in the next chapter that you could try out with anyone willing to cuddle. After that we will go over the Friendly Cuddle Positions. These are recommended for friends, family, and romantic partners depending of course on the comfort of both parties. They are fun, interesting, and allow for all sorts of different interactions. Get creative, and don't be afraid to modify. These positions combined with the modest positions will give you a working repertoire to find solace in a multitude of scenarios. For those of you looking to add a little more intimacy to your cuddling the Affectionate Cuddle Positions are for you. You'll find some quick and easy ways to spice up any relationship, and with these concepts you are bound to gain the closeness that you desire. With the tips and tricks of a real life Professional Cuddler you have in your hands the secrets to cuddling perfection.

Cuddle Positions Legend

Couples & Romantic Partners

Family & Friends

Professional Cuddlers

Parents & Kids

Where to try this position:

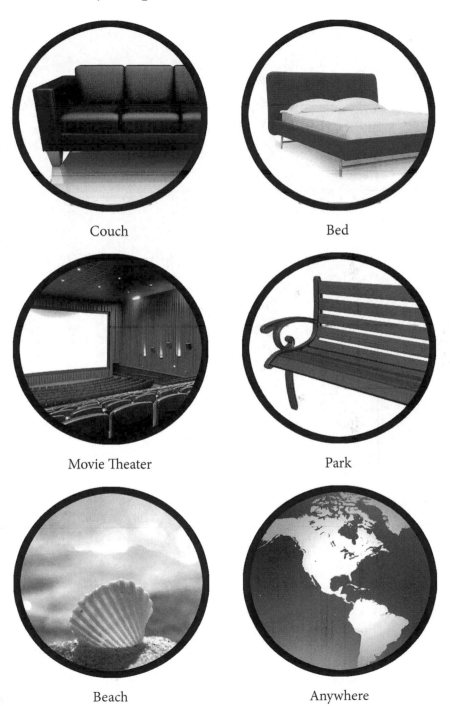

Couch

Bed

Movie Theater

Park

Beach

Anywhere

How long is the position typically comfortable:

Less than five minutes

Less than 15 minutes

Less than 30 minutes

Over an hour

How flexible do I have to be?

Basic Flexibility

Moderate Flexibility

Advanced Flexibility

Modest Cuddle Positions

"Sometimes your only
available transportation
is a leap of faith."
—Margaret Shepard

Go to moves for these Cuddle Personalities:

Anti-Cuddler
Cautious Cuddler

Positions in this Chapter:

The Cloak
The Pyramid
The Back Scratcher
Cleopatra
The Bees Knees
The Tarantino

These positions are intended to allow you to ease into your cuddling while expanding your comfort zone slowly. As you get more comfortable try adding new things to your cuddle time: hand holding, gentle shoulder rubs, soft caresses, fingers that run through the hair of your partner. Communication is key to maintaining your comfort. Make sure you verbalize anything that you are uncomfortable with as it comes up. Remember that you can't expect anyone to read your mind, and body language is not always as clear as we'd like it to be. It is very common and normal for our bodies to make noises, and because it happens to everyone it's nothing to be embarrassed about. If you are concerned about the random tummy rumblings, sounds of breathing, etc. try turning on some music or watching television during your cuddle time.

Keep in mind that even if cuddling just isn't for you, it may be an immense help in improving your relationships and showing your appreciation for those in your life. If you are willing to show your love in the ideal way for your friend, family member, or loved one you will gain their love, respect, and acceptance much easier. This will result in less arguments, more smiles, and hopefully the improved communication will mean the reciprocity required for both of you to feel the love and acceptance you need will shine through. When you have what you need life is amazing, so read on and find some keys to making positive change.

the cloak

"The lust for comfort, that stealthy thing
that enters the house a guest, and then
becomes a host, and then a master."
—Khalil Gibran

Whenever we need a moment to hide from the world there is no better cover than the unconditional love of another. The Cloak is inspired by the need to see the world from a myopic point of view. When things need to be simple and basic. When life needs to just be good. The Cloak provides the sensory response of comforting pressure to help our bodies release serotonin and lift our spirits. To ensure both parties are comfortable I recommend the person on top be no bigger than the person beneath. Have one person start by lying comfortably on their stomach without a pillow and head turned to the side. The second gently lies directly on top of them ensuring the weight of their chest and head are on the mid to upper back. Once full pressure is applied make sure the bottom person is comfortable and their breathing is not diminished.

Tips, Tricks, and Tidbits:

- A small pillow may be used under the hips of the bottom cuddler to help alleviate any low back pain.

- Try bending one knee out to the side to give you more breathing room.

- If the person on top is about the same size it may be best to keep the knees out to the sides to ensure there is not too much strain.

- This position can be very comforting for those who have Autism, ADHD, Asperger's, and many other conditions that rely on sensory input.

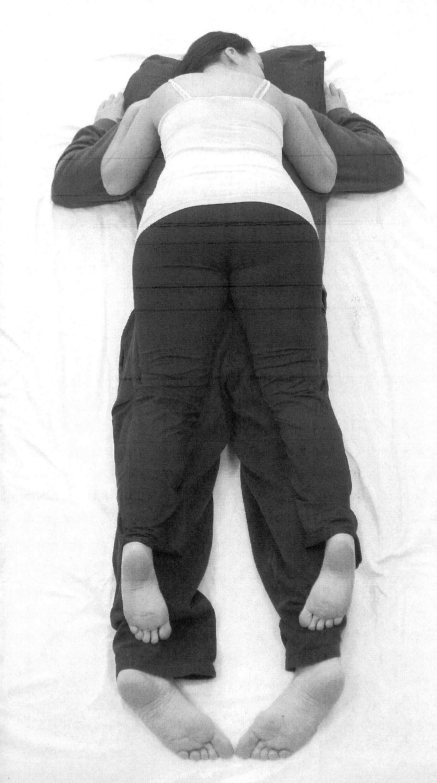

the pyramid

"The pyramid shape is said to hold
many secrets and amazing properties.
One of them is a sense of wonder."
—Vera Nazarian

This has to be one of the most comforting positions. Having the light pressure and security of another upon my back is very soothing. I tend to sleep best in this position, as it allows you that sense of closeness without the discomfort that can come from intertwined arms and legs. For this one start with each person lying down facing away from each other with their heads sharing one pillow or on separate pillows depending on your comfort. Scoot up close to each other so your backs touch from shoulders to tailbone. Legs can go into the fetal position or stretch our a bit in bigger beds. Don't worry if you end up a bit sideways; you can always move your pyramid in the other direction with a quick nudge or gentle request.

Tips, Tricks, and Tidbits

- For romantic partners try this one with bare skin. This is the ultimate luxury when it comes to intimacy without the stress of mixed signals.

- Are you and your cuddle partner opposites when it comes to temperature? If you throw all the covers on top of the chilly person once they are settled you will be able to grab them back when needed without fighting over the blankets.

- Try hugging a pillow to feel surrounded by the blissful soft touch.

the back scratcher

This position is great for napping, lying in bed after waking up, or as a segue to a more intimate position. Start with one person lying comfortably on their stomach and arms up by their head. The second person comes in and lies down along either side resting their head on the arm of the first. This leaves one arm free to gently rub the other's back or give them a good scratch. When it comes to back scratches pressure can be tricky to figure out. I suggest asking your cuddle buddy how hard they would like you to scratch and invite them to tell you as go along if they would like more or less pressure. Another important consideration is the possible roughness of your fingertips. If your nails are sharp or skin is too rough try using a back scratching tool instead.

Tips, Tricks, and Tidbits:

- Use a pillow on top of their arm, or rest your head on the top corner of their back if you are uncomfortable.

- If you haven't had someone scratch your back, give it a try- this one is for everybody to enjoy!

- This is a great position to use in the Summer. Grab an ice pack and help your cuddle buddy cool down. I'm sure they won't mind returning the favor.

cleopatra

"Fool! Don't you see now that I could
have poisoned you a hundred times
had I been able to live without you."
—Cleopatra

This Egyptian Queen is known for having the beauty, wit, and character needed to obtain what she most desired in her life. I believe we all have a little Cleopatra in us, and we should learn to embrace it more often. Let us feel good in who we are and how to get what we need. Let us bask in our own self-worth and live a life of fulfilled desires. When we feel our own needs are satisfied we can help others achieve this too.

For this position, start on a couch or somewhere you will have room to spread out. Have the first person sit upright with one leg out straight along the couch and the other leg bent off the front so there is room for the other person to sit between their legs. The second person then cozies themselves up to the first resting their legs out and torso leaning against the other person.

Tips, Tricks, and Tidbits:

- If the person you are leaning on is not comfortable, first try raising or lowering yourself to find a better position, and if all else fails grab a pillow to put between you.

- Don't be afraid to have fun with this one. Grab a bunch of grapes or some popcorn and feed your Cleopatra as you lounge.

- This one is perfect to include with the little ones. Grab a pillow and a book to read. You've got an afternoon perfect for a story and nap time together.

the bees knees

"Put your heart, mind, and soul
into even your smallest acts...
This is the secret of success."
—Swami Sivananda

Sometimes the simplest things can be the greatest comfort; The smell of grandma's peanut butter cookies, singing along to a favorite on the radio, or laughing about old times with a friend you haven't seen in far too long. We never know what may be the next thing to trigger a good memory or a nice feeling, so pay attention. Look for the little things, and when life give you lemons, make lemonade. When life gives you knees though, make a pillow. Start by having one person lie down on their side with their knees slightly bent forward, and steadily balanced. The second person starts by placing their head on the knees (or legs near the knee if more comfortable) of the other person and aligning themselves so their partner may do the same. It make take a little adjusting, but once you've got it, it's quite nice.

Tips, Tricks, and Tidbits:

- Major height differences can be a bit challenging to line up, but try bending the knees more or less, moving closer or further apart, or up or down on the bed to find the right angle. I promise, it's there.

- A thin pillow placed between your knees and wrapped around so it can be used by your partner as well is a great way to create further ease.

- From this position you can play the Drawing Game described on page 53. Make sure you use appropriate areas for whomever you are with. Below the knee or on the arms is great for friends and kids.

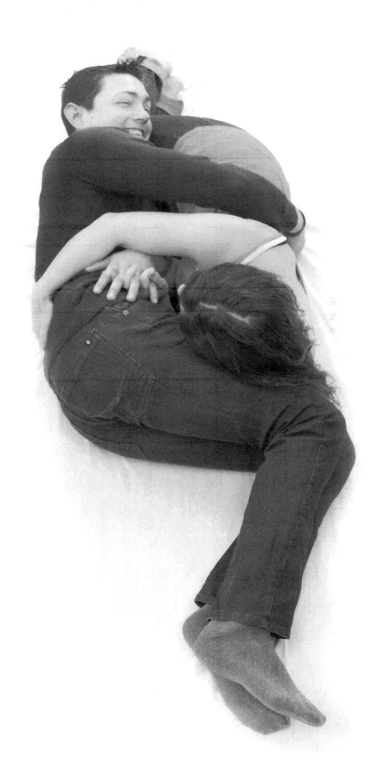

the tarantino

"I'm not shying away from my obsession with feet. If you think about the directors that have been accused of being foot-crazy, it would have been Alfred Hitchcock, Buñuel and Samuel Fuller. I am in pretty good company. It suggests they were pretty good filmmakers because they knew where to put their camera."
—Quentin Tarantino

The simple honesty spoken by this man is refreshing. So few of us speak our minds in such an open and direct way. I think it's fantastic. Be who you are, say what you mean, and feel good about it because in this world there will never be another you. Life truly is what we make of it, so why not get what you want? If you are anything like Tarantino this position may be for you. Give it a try and see what you think. Start by having one person sit up leaning against a pillow. This person will then bend their knees with their feet flat. The second person comes in near their feet and sits below their knees (the first person's legs go to the sides). Bring the second person's feet to rest on the chest of the other, and arms can rest on top of their knees. This position allows for the space needed to keep some of us comfortable while still allowing us contact (and maybe a foot rub if we are lucky).

Tips, Tricks, and Tidbits:

- This can be a great way to stretch your back while getting some cuddle time. Try doing some spinal flexions like the Cat/Cow positions in yoga.

- Try chatting with your partner or having them read out loud while you rub their feet. Sometimes all it takes is a little face-to-face attention to make your day better.

- If your flexibility is lacking try resting your feet to the side of their hips in a mirrored position of each other. You will still be able to massage their feet or legs without the strain.

"Life begins at the end of your comfort zone."
—Neale Donald Walsch

Friendly Cuddle Positions

"One of the most beautiful qualities
of true friendship is to understand
and to be understood."
—Lucius Annaeus Seneca

Go to moves for these Cuddle Personalities:
Conventional Cuddler
Outgoing Cuddler

Positions in this Chapter:

The Cinema
Mama Bear/Papa Bear
Catch Up
The Pineapple
Nesting Dolls
Blooming Lotus

You already have the basics down, but are looking to explore some options to make cuddling more fun and interesting. With the positions in this chapter you will discover some options that may be new to you. They are designed to be comfortable in a variety of scenarios, and may give you the desire to expand who is on your cuddle list. Many of them can be interactive, giving you a chance to chat, play games, or read together. There is a different position for every mood. With your skill try lots of them in this chapter as well as the others to explore your talent and enhance your sense of touch.

No matter your gender there can be difficulties when it comes to incorporating platonic touch in your life. With groups where even hugs are limited it may seem impossible to gain the acceptance that touch can so easily provide. Rest assured though, that if you pay close attention and are willing to try new things you will soon start to feel safe reaching out for more of what you need. If all else fails there are cuddle groups that you can join and Professional Cuddlers that are popping up all over if you prefer one on one time. So often in our lives we simply go without because we are afraid to ask. When it comes to basic needs like touch you should always feel good about finding ways to reach out and fulfill this need in a positive way. The proceeding chapter will give you the platonic options to help you connect. After practicing the concepts in this book you will have the talent, touch, and communication skills needed to create your perfect cuddle scenario. The following pages will help you hone in on the ways to get there.

the cinema

"For it was not into my ear you whispered,
but into my heart. It was not my
lips you kissed, but my soul."
—Judy Garland

Movies can take us on a roller coaster ride of emotions without leaving our living room. Whenever possible, it is nice to go through that ride with someone by your side. With The Cinema, you can share all those moments (but still be able to get up easily for snacks or bathroom breaks). Start in a seated position next to each other. One person will then turn themselves toward the other bringing their knees up besides the legs of the other, head on their shoulder, and arm in arm. Another great thing about this position is that many of us are warmer or cooler than our partners. With The Cinema, the cooler person can bundle up in their own blanket before cuddling up to avoid overheating the other.

Tips, Tricks, and Tidbits:

- For me this is the best way to watch a movie. I get to grab onto someone's arm and feel close, but also have freedom of movement to avoid getting a kink in my neck.

- Try this in a chair or sofa that reclines and has a foot rest for maximum comfort.

- Make sure you find a comfy set up that works for you as quickly as possible. When you are cuddling for a movie it's important not to move too much because you may diminish your cuddle buddy's movie experience.

- For the person being leaned upon don't be afraid to reciprocate the touch you receive with hand holding or reaching out for their leg, but be warned- if you put your arm around them you risk getting stuck that way.

mama bear/papa bear

*"A mother's arms are made
of tenderness and children
sleep soundly in them."*
—Victor Hugo

This is my go to position for putting someone at ease. Allowing someone to simply melt into you can take the weight of the world off their shoulders. I find that size is not a big issue with this position, and even someone tiny like myself can be great at being the bear. It's like wearing a hug. To start, set up a pillow or two on a bed and have one person make themselves comfortable in a seated position legs apart. Have the second person carefully glide up into the space created for them being careful not to sit too close if there is a male (Papa Bear) in the seated position to start. Lean back to rest your head and torso on the Bear, and simply relax. With a bear in the room you are never alone.

Tips, Tricks, and Tidbits:

- For most partners I recommend using a pillow between you for maximum comfort.

- If the person in the back raises their knees this can be a perfect position for a calf and/or foot massage for them. The front person can also benefit from a gentle shoulder massage as well.

- This is a great position for reading to little ones. They can hold the book and turn the pages as you read so that they feel involved as well.

- Watching movies like this is a great way to enjoy the luxury of a few hours to relax.

catch up

"Too often we underestimate the power of a touch, a smile, a kind word, a listening ear, an honest compliment, or the smallest act of caring, all of which have the potential to turn a life around."
—Leo Buscaglia

Life seems to rush by at an exponentially faster rate. There are never enough hours in the day, and when you finally get a chance to take a breath it's nice to find a few minutes to catch up with a friend, family member, or loved one. This position allows us to catch up by slowing things down and getting cozy. To start have one person sit in a comfortable position on a couch or bed. The other person will lie their head in the lap of the first facing up to look at them. Legs for the person lying down may be laid out flat, or knees bent depending on comfort. The Catch Up will allow you to bond over reassuring touch and conversation.

Tips, Tricks, and Tidbits:

- Running your fingers through the hair of the person lying down as you cuddle is a great way comfort them and show you care.

- As a rule of thumb I like to make the seated person the listener and the person lying down the talker. This way you both get a chance to talk without the concern of being interrupted.

- If you are done chatting and want to watch a movie have the person lying down turn to their side so you are both facing the same direction and press play.

- This is perfect for trying out a guided meditation. Have the seated person make one up and then switch. Before you know it the world will feel a lot less stressful.

the pineapple

"Be who you are and say how you feel
cause those who mind don't matter
and those who matter don't mind."
—Dr Seuss

When we first came up with this position I was with my friend Dori at a party. I was lying beside her and said "I have no idea why, but I want to call this one The Pineapple." Her response was "Logically, I don't get it, but emotionally this is totally a pineapple." We all laughed, but once I did a little research I discovered that the pineapple has been a symbol of hospitality for hundreds of years. What better name for a cuddle position! For this one have one person lie on a couch sideways with their head resting on the arm of the sofa and their legs apart. Once they are comfortable join them by lying on your side in the space created with your head on their chest and knees slightly tucked. They can then comfortably rest their leg on top of you to complete the position.

Tips, Tricks, and Tidbits:

- If you are worried about getting sensitive areas squished add a pillow to the mix to ensure you have enough space.

- A bed works just as well as long as you use a couple of pillows to lean on.

- I find one of the most comforting sounds to be a heartbeat. This position allows you access to listen in. Take heed in the quiet for a moment and relax to the soothing sound of life.

- This is another great position to catch up on a tv show, have a chat, or play one of the listening games from the Communication chapter.

nesting dolls

> "I know there is strength in the
> differences between us. I know
> there is comfort where we overlap."
> —Ani DiFranco

Sometimes it's nice to feel enshrouded with love. We all have our ways of escaping when reality gets to be a bit too much. When done in a positive way this is a healthy part of life, but many of us retreat to a place where we must go through our issues alone. A good book, a glass of wine, or a tv show are all fine, but if you want to grow and truly thrive I would like to suggest when those moments hit try Nesting Dolls instead. Encompass yourself with love and feel secure in the trust and protection it provides. Start with one person sitting sideways on a couch nice and tall with legs apart. The second person sits in the space created and wraps their arms around as they pull their knees in and flatten their feet. Once they are comfortable, the first person can then lean into the second and wrap their arms around as the perfect armor against all things troublesome.

Tips, Tricks, and Tidbits:

- Try lightly rubbing the back of the person in front for added assurance.

- While tickling may seem fun, I would discourage it in this position as their elbows may end up instinctively retracting right into you. That's a reaction that pulls us back to reality a bit too quickly.

- If this position is used on a soft bed make sure the person in the back is seated nice and tall- on the sits bones if at all possible to help avoid back pain.

blooming lotus

*"Life is made up, not of great sacrifices or duties, but of
little things, in which smiles and kindness, and small obligations
given habitually, are what preserve the heart and secure comfort."*
—Humphry Davy

My ego comes from the relentless pursuit of my happiness by my
Mother. She literally made me an award for Christmas one year that
proclaimed I was "Best at Everything." She is my guide for how to
treat others in this world. She would never tell me what to do, but instead simply
leads by example. Every act has intent and care put into it. This has been deeply
instilled in me, and if I end up being 10% of who my Mom has turned out to
be, I will be the happiest girl. The Blooming Lotus is inspired by the idea that
those little moments where you can sit down and give someone your undivided
attention will leave a lasting impression on their soul in a beautiful way. Sit facing
each other close enough that you can wrap your legs around one another, and
bring your hands to rest on whomever's knees are on top. This allows you to
enjoy the simple things in life like looking in someone's eyes and seeing them
smile.

Tips, Tricks, and Tidbits:

- Try the Thankful Game in this position. Go back and forth saying things you
  are thankful for.

- You will need some flexibility for this to be comfortable, so try stretching
  your hamstrings before you start. This will allow your body to ease into it
  easier.

- One of the funnest nights I've had in a long time was playing a face painting
  game with a friend. This position works great for that. Take turns applying
  one finger's worth of paint to the others face with no mirrors around. Even
  feeling the paint go on I had no clue what it was going to look like. So great!

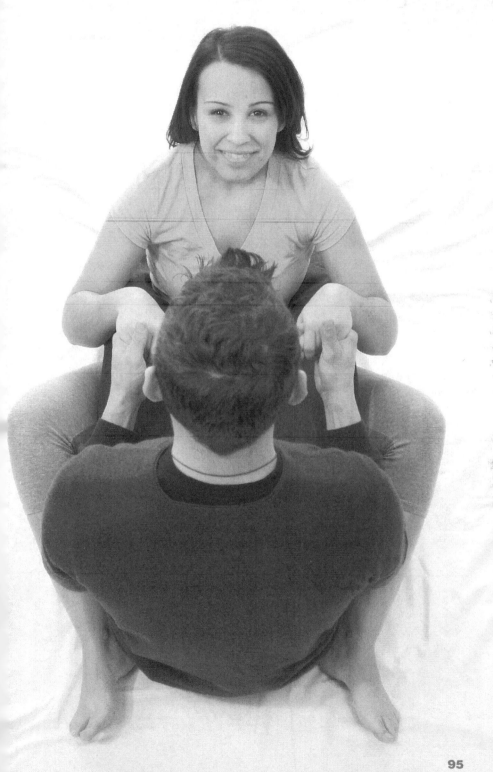

"It is the sweet, simple things of life
which are the real ones after all."
—Laura Ingalls Wilder

Affectionate Cuddle Positions

"Being deeply loved by someone
gives you strength, while loving
someone deeply gives you courage."
—Lao Tzu

Go to moves for these Cuddle Personalities:

Ultimate Cuddle Bug
Outgoing Cuddler

Positions in this Chapter:

Honeymoon
Gemini
Superhero
Warm Embrace
The Side Pocket
Tandem Bike
Melchior

If you are lucky enough to have a special person in your life to be romantic towards these positions are made for you! All of these embraces are designed with the idea that closeness is desired between you and your partner. These positions are a bit more intimate than the rest, and allow you to really connect with those you hold (or who hold you). I am not a fan of gender roles when it comes to cuddling, and I believe we can all benefit from being the cuddler as well as the cuddlee. In my business I have yet to find someone who doesn't benefit from being the little spoon once in a while. Explore something new, and you may find a kind of comfort you never knew you could have.

When you and your partner are driven by different levels of touch you may, even with your advanced skill level, find that your touch needs are not being met. I highly encourage you to verbalize your needs in a well thought out and non-confrontational manner. I find most of the time that I do this best through e-mail. When I get to sit and carefully craft the right words to explain how I feel rather than try to perfect it off the cuff I know that I have a much better chance of getting a positive result. Do what is right for you, and if you know someone who is lacking in the touch department don't hesitate to reach out and offer your hand. The positions in this chapter from a dear friend or loved one can be the difference between feeling alone and feeling loved. Turn the page, grab your cuddle buddy, and get back to happy.

honeymoon

"I want to be very close to someone
I respect and admire and have somebody
who feels the same way about me."
—Richard Bach

Love is an incredible thing. The capacity for love is endless, and does not diminish by the number of people you love. There are many types of love: romantic, maternal, spiritual, unconditional, puppy, etc. The list goes on and on. We love in different ways and for different reasons, but the fact that we love is undeniable. It is what life is made of. Love is created in the smallest of gestures and the grandest of thoughts. The Honeymoon is a great paradigm of love. It allows you in a small and sweet way to show your care for another while providing the time to daydream about the grandest of things. Begin by having one person lie on their back and one on their side next to each other. The one on their side brings up their knees as the other does the same to create a double cradle of sorts. You can wrap your arms around each other and hold on tight. Pretty soon you'll feel the love of the world encompassing you, keeping you safe and warm.

Tips, Tricks, and Tidbits:

- For a true Honeymoon feel try having the bottom cuddler bring their arm under the legs of the other as if they were carrying the bride over the threshold. And this time you won't hit their head on the door frame!

- Show your love through your touch. The more touch you give and receive the better your sense of touch becomes, and the more beneficial the experience will feel.

- Sometimes it's nice to use a moment like this to express a small gesture of your love. Try verbally praising your partner with compliments, and hopefully they will do the same.

gemini

"It is not our purpose to become each other;
it is to recognize each other, to learn to
see the other and honor him for what he is."
—Hermann Hesse

This horoscope symbol is often pictured as two that become one. Sort of the two sides of a coin scenario; they are two distinct pieces of the same thing. The Gemini is all about recognition and acceptance of the individual as well as the synchronicities that bind us together. When we are strong enough in our own sense of self to contribute a piece of ourselves to the collective, the world around us becomes stronger, better. It is about knowing that if you have a whole pie and you share a piece, it will in no way diminish the satisfaction of the piece you are eating, and in fact, being able to share in the benefit of others is greater than the enjoyment you would get from keeping the whole pie to yourself. Start by lying on your sides facing each other with your arms in front of you. Scoot close enough together to intertwine your legs and arms as two become one.

Tips, Tricks, and Tidbits:

- Try different positions with your arms for a personalized experience. Rest your head in the crook of your bottom arm, or place your bottom arm along your side your back as you turn your body slightly toward your partner.

- The Staring game is great from this angle. Try looking staring into each other's eyes without talking for a few moments. The respect, acceptance, and understanding you may find can go a long way in our well being.

- If your partner is a Gemini they will gain greatly from all aspects of conversation. Try to find a topic or fact to discuss and find them light up with a sense of wonder and curiosity that will surely bring you both joy.

superhero

"Hard times don't create heroes.
It is during the hard times when
the 'hero' within us is revealed."
—Bob Riley

S pooning is the classic cuddle position. It's the go to move for most cuddle sessions because it's comfortable for just about everybody no matter your size, shape, or age. The Superhero is my version of the classic Spoon. The difference is that with my position you avoid the trapped arm issue. With this position the "hug and roll" actually works. To get into this position start by having the "little spoon" lie down on their side. The "big spoon" can then scoot in next to them, but instead of putting their arm out as a pillow, use a real pillow and extend that arm straight up. The big spoon can then curl their top arm around the little spoon like a superhero would when flying someone to safety.

Tips, Tricks, and Tidbits:

- If your arm gets tired from being extended up try resting it behind your head.

- To make this position even more comfortable try placing a pillow between your knees.

- Try both positions for a new perspective. I love falling asleep as the big spoon because I can roll away and come back whenever I want without disturbing my partner.

warm embrace

"When you look at me,
when you think of me,
I am in paradise."
—William Makepeace Thackeray

When the road seems long, the debt seems high. and you feel like you're barely getting by. When you go through your day with no time to play. You want to smile, but can only pout. This is not what life is about. Take my hand. I understand. Life is not a chase, and yes, I can see you need some breathing space. Let's walk in the sand, hand in hand. And if you still can't come out from your hiding place at least let me join you in a Warm Embrace. This position is there for those moments when you need to know you are not alone. Hold each other tight, and just feel okay for a moment. Start by lying down facing each other and legs out straight. One person can then move their head up and turn their face to the side allowing them to rest their cheek on the shoulder of the other as your arms embrace one another.

Tips, Tricks, and Tidbits:

- If you have long hair try to bring it to your side so it doesn't completely cover the person you are cuddling.

- Try this position with one person bringing their leg on top for a full body cuddle!

- A light shoulder rub or caress on the mid to upper back can be very relaxing. Give it a try and feel the stress melt away.

- If your body gets uncomfortable holding this position try bringing your head down to the pillow and resting curled up under your partner's chin.

- Don't be afraid to press your torsos close together. Closing the gap to create that puzzle piece fit feels great.

the side pocket

"Electric communication will never be a substitute
for the face of someone who with their soul
encourages another person to be brave and true."
—Charles Dickens

The Side Pocket always makes me feel like I have the safety of home even when I'm far away. No matter where I am, when I'm in your arms the rest of the world can disappear for a moment. For me, this is what life is truly about. No matter the size of the person I cuddle with I feel like this space was created just for me. It's always a perfect fit. Start by having one person lie on their back with one arm out wide. The second person can then cozy up by lying on their side facing their partner. They then press their body alongside the first and rest their head on a small pillow or the shoulder there. Once you are both in place, the arm that was out wide can come in to rest on the other's back for a final movement that locks in that sense of well-being.

Tips, Tricks, and Tidbits:

- My secret for this position is for the person on their side to bring their lower hand behind them rather than in front. It can then meet the hand on their back and create a sense of perfect puzzle pieces. Magic!

- If I feel the need to sleep in this position, I will modify it by lying on my side and wrapping my arms around the arm closest to me rather than lying on top of it. This allows me to roll away when I need to without disturbing the other person.

- A very light spray of perfume or cologne at the top of your shirt can creates a lovely way to help form a stronger memory of that moment. It's the perfect spot to enhance the senses for the person on their side.

tandem bike

"For beautiful eyes, look for the good in others;
for beautiful lips, speak only words of kindness; and for
poise, walk with the knowledge that you are never alone."
—Audrey Hepburn

The Tandem Bike was created as a hybrid of the spoon to allow lots of touch and talk time. For me that sense of envelopment is so soothing, and when you add in the ability to converse easily I find that this position is one of my favorites for early mornings or late nights with my special someone. Start in the basic spoon position and have the little spoon rotate to about a 45 degree angle. Next the little spoon will bring out their bottom knee as if they were on a bike, and the big spoon can then bring their top leg across bent at the knee to mirror this movement. This position is so comfortable you may never want to ride a real bike again.

Tips, Tricks, and Tidbits:

- In platonic cuddle partners ensure the comfort of both parties by having the little spoon guide the hand of the big spoon to the arm or shoulder.

- This is a position like the Superhero where it may be a good idea to keep your arm free. Try Using the crook of your arm as a pillow for more comfort.

- For height differences of more than a few inches it may be best to keep the taller person as the big spoon or have the taller person turn to a flatter plane.

- If your back hurts when you are on your side this is a great alternative to using a pillow between your knees. Pressure's off with no extra tools needed.

melchior

"At the heart of personality is the need
to feel a sense of being lovable without
having to qualify for that acceptance."
—Paul Tournier

M elchior is a fluffy gray cat with a striking wit and shameless self-indulgence. Incessant meowing for food or to go outside, and his constant need for attention make him seem much more like a dog than a cat at times. His attention to detail is astounding; if you put something important down he will immediately lie down on it so you will have to pet him if you want it back. His owner and my roommate, Melon, is the quintessential embodiment of unconditional love with Mel (and pretty much everyone she runs into). She is the perfect parent for this catdog, and doesn't mind at all when he pulls a Mel and sprawls out across her as she tries to work. Start with one person lying flat and have the second person start sitting on their knees next to the first. They can then drape themselves across the first person in a leisurely way resting their head on the chest or shoulder of the other as they find a comfortable position for their legs.

Tips, Tricks, and Tidbits:

- This position is great when you need a little love. Thrusting yourself upon your partner will certainly gain their attention and fill your need for affection.

- I am not much for tv watching, but sometimes my cuddle buddies are. This is the perfect compromise- have your partner prop themselves up with an extra pillow. They can watch the tube while I get in my cuddle time.

- Sometimes I find myself more comfortable lying on the shoulder closer to me. Bring out your inner cat and go with what feels right in the moment.

afterword

be who you want to be

> "Find the love you seek, by first finding the love
> within yourself. Learn to rest in that place
> within you that is your true home."
> —Ravi Shankar

I live my life based on being real with people, speaking up and never holding back. No matter who you are, what you need, or where you are going, life is richer when lived in concert with those around you. We can do it alone, certainly, but to truly thrive we must learn the bravery of letting go. Allowing us to contribute to each other creates value. Why live in mono when stereo can be exceptional? Finding fault is human. Finding strength in our differences is even more so. We are incredible beings, each and every one of us. We have within us the ability to impact not only ourselves, but the world around us. When we work together our ability to bring a positive shift comes into focus.

Each one of us must feel fulfilled before we can devote our lives to others. If there is only oxygen in the tank for one, splitting it will only cause you both to perish twice as fast. The tools described here are meant to help us find what we need to feel whole. Like a chef and his knife, a pilot and her plane or astronauts and their spacesuits, we must have the tools that allow us to complete our desired actions. Everyone needs something in their life: love, attention, respect, touch. No matter what it is you need, the keys to obtaining it lies in your ability to understand, communicate, and act upon your desires. If we need something. it is completely up to us to make it happen. We cannot rely on others to read our minds or be proactive in finding what we need without guidance from us. We are all guilty of this from time to time, but let's make a pact to avoid that feeling as often as possible.

My hope with this book is to give you the tools you need to take that next step. Take action. Make something happen for yourself that you didn't know you could. Life is full of ups and downs. Contrast is what makes life interesting. The difference is that you can do the same thing over and over again with the same results — or you can make a change. You can fight for what you need and begin anew. Life can be what you want it to be. You can be who you want to be. If I can teach you anything I hope it is this:

You are loved.
You are accepted.
You are worthy.
And you can do something to prove it.

photo credits

T.he Cloak
Samantha Hess and Rob Ems

The Pyramid
Samantha Hess and Jessica Hostetler

The Back Scratcher
Samantha Hess and Preston Yates

Cleopatra
Samantha Hess and Jessica Hostetler

The Bees Knees
Emilee Yaakola and Josh Sabraw

The Tarantino
Samantha Hess and Tony Lintz

The Cinema
Tony Lintz and KaiKani Seven Vanity

Mama Bear/Papa Bear
Samantha Hess and Preston Yates

Catch Up
Samantha Hess and Tony Lintz

The Pineapple
Samantha Hess and Jessica Hostetler

Nesting Dolls
Samantha Hess and KaiKani Seven Vanity

Blooming Lotus
Samantha Hess and Josh Sabraw

Honeymoon
Susan Paul and John Paul

Gemini
Samantha Hess and KaiKani Seven Vanity

Superhero
Samantha Hess and John Paul

Warm Embrace
Samantha Hess and KaiKani Seven Vanity

The Side Pocket
Samantha Hess and Tony Lintz

Tandem Bike
Samantha Hess and Rob Ems

Melchior
Samantha Hess and Susan Paul

acknowledgements

Art Directors
Jessica Hostetler
Kellie Long
Melissa McLain

Book Design
Chris Vetter

Contributing Editors
Robert Ems
Jason Garcia
Gretchen Lindemann
Chris Vetter
Elizabeth Yates

Cuddling Photography
Kelly McLain

Outdoor Photography
Carla Axtman
Joe Wilson

Photo Editors
Carla Axtman
Chris Vetter

Researchers
Robert Long
Samantha Hess
Chris Vetter

Special Thanks
Sean Dougherty
Terry Galliher
Andres Gomez
Daniel Hess
Nicholas Hill
Natasha Lunt
Meghan Mendenhall
Laura Olson
Baby Leland Foundation
The Ed Forman Show
Oregon Food Bank

about the author

Samantha Hess is on a mission to change lives. As a professional cuddler, she helps her clients rediscover the power of human intimacy. Seen by over 16 million people in interviews across the globe, she is the leading expert on the healing power of touch. Samantha is about to launch the most visible cuddling center in North America and tour the United States promoting her debut book. By the end of 2014, she will reach over 30 million people with her message of hope, renewal and empowerment.

Big things come in small packages. Samantha is barely five feet and weighs 115 pounds, but her stature in the cuddling movement grows taller every day. A 30 year-old native Oregonian, she earned advanced fitness certifications and is an expert on kinesiology and the workings of the human body. Her scholarly approach to the science and psychology behind cuddling is unmatched.

"Cuddling is more than a service Samantha provides," said *Inside Portland Magazine* editor Chris Vetter. "She wants to break down the boundaries that prevent us from embracing each other. She is a loving presence in the world, determined to help others reach their full potential. Her book *Touch: The Power of Human Connection* is on track to become a classic, inspiring people to enhance their self-esteem and achieve deeper intimacy."

"Samantha offers a service nearly everyone on the planet needs," said Washington student Robert Long. "We can count on two hands the number of people in the United States who cuddle for a living. In a nation of over 300 million people that seems almost impossible, but this industry is brand new. Samantha approaches her craft with sincerity and sophistication. Her understanding of the science behind human touch is what distinguishes her in the marketplace. She is a relaxation therapist, a counselor, a comforting friend and a powerful voice reminding us to deepen our connections to each other."

"Samantha Hess makes a difference for others," said Portland executive Kimberly Schleiger. "Her work with the Oregon Food Bank and the Baby Leland Foundation speaks to her character. Despite the pressures of creating a new company, she shows up for her charity work every week without fail. Her selflessness and sincerity make her a role model."

In her spare time, Samantha enjoys dancing, hiking, cooking, floating the river, reading out loud with friends and spending time with family.

Cuddle Up ♥ *To Me*

Visit our retail location in Portland, Oregon

For more information visit cuddleuptome.com

Made in the USA
Columbia, SC
15 April 2021